Spelunking Scripture:
The Passion of Christ in the Synoptic Gospels
Exploring Important Passages of the Bible

BRUCE C. SALMON

© 2024
Published in the United States by Nurturing Faith, Macon, GA.
Nurturing Faith is a book imprint of Good Faith Media (goodfaithmedia.org).
Library of Congress Cataloging-in-Publication Data is available.

ISBN: 978-1-63528-247-4

All rights reserved. Printed in the United States of America.

Unless otherwise noted, all scripture quotes are from *New Revised Standard Version* Bible: Anglicized Edition, copyright © 1989, 1995 National Council of the Churches of Christ in the United States of America. Used by permission. All rights reserved worldwide.

Where noted, scripture quotes are from *Holy Bible*. New Living Translation (NLT). Copyright © 1996, 2004, 2015 by Tyndale House Foundation. Used by permission of Tyndale House Publishers, Inc., Carol Stream, IL, 60188. All rights reserved. Also from *The Learning Bible: Contemporary English Version* (CEV). New York: American Bible Society, 2000.

Cover image by falco from Pixabay.

Contents

Introduction v

Chapter 1: The Conspiracy against Jesus
(Matt 26:1-5; Mark 14:1-2; Luke 22:1-2) 1

Chapter 2: The Anointing at Bethany
(Matt 26:6-13; Mark 14:3-9) 5

Chapter 3: Judas Agrees to Betray Jesus
(Matt 26:14-16; Mark 14:10-11; Luke 22:3-6) 9

Chapter 4: Preparation for the Passover
(Matt 26:17-19; Mark 14:12-16; Luke 22:7-13) 15

Chapter 5: The Traitor
(Matt 26:20-25; Mark 14:17-21; Luke 22:14, 21-23) 21

Chapter 6: The Institution of the Lord's Supper
(Matt 26:26-29; Mark 14:22-25; Luke 22:15-20) 25

Chapter 7: Peter's Denial Predicted
(Matt 26:30-35; Mark 14:26-31; Luke 22:31-34, 39+) 29

Chapter 8: Jesus in Gethsemane
(Matt 26:36-46; Mark 14:32-42; Luke 22:40-46) 35

Chapter 9: Jesus Taken Captive
(Matt 26:47-56; Mark 14:43-52; Luke 22:47-53) 39

Chapter 10: Jesus Before the Council; Peter's Denial
(Matt 26:57-75; Mark 14:53-72; Luke 22:54-71) 45

Chapter 11: Jesus Delivered to Pilate
(Matt 27:1-2; Mark 15:1; Luke 23:1+) 49

Chapter 12: The Death of Judas
(Matt 27:3-10) 53

Chapter 13: The Trial Before Pilate
(Matt 27:11-14; Mark 15:2-5; Luke 23:2-5) 57

Chapter 14: Jesus Before Herod
(Luke 23:6-16) 61

Chapter 15: The Sentence of Death
(Matt 27:15-26; Mark 15:6-15; Luke 23:17-25) 65

Chapter 16: The Mocking by the Soldiers
(Matt 27:27-31; Mark 15:16-20) 71

Chapter 17: Simon of Cyrene Carries Jesus's Cross
(Matt 27:32; Mark 15:21; Luke 23:26-32) 77

Chapter 18: The Crucifixion
  (Matt 27:33-44; Mark 15:22-32; Luke 23:33-43) 83
Chapter 19: The Death on the Cross
  (Matt 27:45-56; Mark 15:33-41; Luke 23:44-49) 89
Chapter 20: The Burial of Jesus
  (Matt 27:57-61; Mark 15:42-47; Luke 23:50-56) 95
Chapter 21: The Guard at the Tomb
  (Matt 27:62-66) 99
Addendum: The Passion Story in John
  (John 13–19) 103

Bibliography 113

About the Author 115

Introduction

On Saturday, January 8, 2000, I lost my entire professional library to a fire that destroyed Village Baptist Church in Bowie, Maryland. I should say the building was destroyed by fire; the church was not destroyed. Investigators concluded that the fire started from an electrical short in the wiring in my church office. All the books in my study provided plenty of fuel for the fire. I lost almost everything—books, pastoral records, marriage licenses, funeral documents, sermons, Bible studies I had led, diplomas, my ordination certificate, my license to the ministry, photos, my pulpit robe, my baptismal robe, a suit and tie, shoes, my computer, my printer, my telephone, pictures on the walls, and memorabilia from more than twenty-five years of pastoral service.

The only book remaining from my library of 3,000-plus volumes was a Bible I had taken home with me the night before. Because a book allowance was included in the church budget, I had added books to my library over the years. Frankly, books are essential for a pastor's ministry. Sermon preparation requires study, and books are essential for understanding and interpreting the biblical texts and applying them to modern life.

Once word got out that a pastor had lost his entire theological library, donations began coming my way. Friends and former seminary classmates sent me books, and even some people I did not know offered to help. There was also a provision in the church's insurance policy to cover losses of personal items. The only stipulation was that I had to document the lost books, and the fire destroyed all my records of book purchases. I spent many weeks trying to remember the destroyed books and compiling a list for the insurance company.

Slowly, as the church building was reconstructed, I began reconstructing my pastoral library. Some of it came from donations I received. One former seminary classmate who was no longer in the ministry sent me boxes of books, including many of our seminary textbooks. A retired Cooperative Baptist Fellowship (CBF) field personnel member whom I had never met heard about my loss and sent me a set of Bible dictionaries. Donations also came from the library at my home church, Broadway Baptist Church in Fort Worth, Texas.

Over time I began to rebuild my library by purchasing commentary sets, Bible dictionaries, and other reference books. One book that I purchased was *Gospel Parallels: A Comparison of the Synoptic Gospels* by Burton H. Throckmorton Jr. to replace the copy that had been destroyed in the fire. It was the fifth edition of Throckmorton's classic, based on the New Revised Standard Version of the Synoptic Gospels.

In his preface to the fifth edition, Throckmorton wrote that he had begun work on the book in the summer of 1946, "without air conditioning," at Union Theological Seminary in New York. It was also the year that the Revised Standard Version of the New Testament was published. That first edition of *Gospel Parallels* was published in 1949. By the publication of the fifth edition in 1992, the book had gone through four editions and thirty-five printings, becoming widely used throughout the English-speaking world. The publication of the New Revised Standard Version of the New Testament in 1990 prompted Throckmorton to revise his work once again for the fifth edition, this time based on the NRSV.

Recently, as I reviewed Throckmorton's *Gospel Parallels*, I noticed how he grouped the parallel scripture texts and labeled each passage. For example, he labeled the parallel passages in Matthew 26:1-5, Mark 14:1-2, and Luke 22:1-2 as "The Conspiracy against Jesus." His labeling of each group of parallel passages inspired me to follow his index in the fifth edition of *Gospel Parallels* for this study, focusing on the Passion Narrative, indices 231–252, found on pages 181–204. I am using Throckmorton's title for each passage of parallels. So chapter 1 of this book is titled "The Conspiracy against Jesus," which is 231 in Throckmorton's index. Chapter 2 is "The Anointing at Bethany," which is 232 in *Gospel Parallels*. And so on. In many cases, there are parallels of the passage in all three Synoptic Gospels. In some cases, the passage is not in all three Gospels but in one or two. In each chapter, I discuss the passage in whichever Gospel(s) it occurs.

My method is to introduce each passage, discuss the relationship between the parallel(s), and then interpret the passage through a sermon based on one of the Gospel occurrences. The goal is to follow the Passion Narrative through the presentations in Matthew, Mark, and Luke and seek to understand the messages for our lives.

The passion of Christ is the story of his suffering and death. The word "passion" comes from the Latin *passio*, which means "suffering." All four Gospels make Jesus's passion the culminating focus of his life. Of course, the resurrection is the conclusion to the story. As I say in the introduction to *Spelunking Scripture: Easter* (Nurturing Faith, 2022), "The resurrection of Jesus is the linchpin of the Christian faith." But without the passion, there would have been no resurrection. So the passion of Christ is the crux of the Christian faith.

Beyond the Gospels, much of the rest of the New Testament includes interpretations of what the crucifixion of Christ means for us. Consider these verses:

In 1 Corinthians 1:17-18 Paul wrote, "For Christ did not send me to baptize but to proclaim the gospel, and not with eloquent wisdom, so that the cross of Christ might not be emptied of its power. For the message about the cross is foolishness to those who are perishing, but to us who are being saved it is the power of God."

In Galatians 2:19-20 Paul wrote, "I have been crucified with Christ; and it is no longer I who live, but it is Christ who lives in me."

In Galatians 6:14 Paul wrote, "May I never boast of anything except the cross of our Lord Jesus Christ, by which the world has been crucified to me, and I to the world."

In Ephesians 2:15-16 Paul wrote, "He has abolished the law with its commandments and ordinances, so that he might create in himself one new humanity in place of the two, thus making peace, and might reconcile both groups to God in one body through the cross, thus putting to death that hostility through it."

In Philippians 2:7-11 Paul wrote, "And being found in human form, he humbled himself and became obedient to the point of death—even death on a cross. Therefore God also highly exalted him and gave him the name that is above every name, so that at the name of Jesus every knee should bend, in heaven and on earth and under the earth, and every tongue should confess that Jesus Christ is Lord, to the glory of God the Father."

In Colossians 1:19-20 Paul wrote, "For in him all the fullness of God was pleased to dwell, and through him God was pleased to reconcile to himself all things, whether on earth or in heaven, by making peace through the blood of his cross."

Hebrews 12:1-2 says, "Therefore, since we are surrounded by so great a cloud of witnesses, let us also lay aside every weight and the sin that clings so closely, and let us run with perseverance the race that is set before us, looking to Jesus the pioneer and perfecter of our faith, who for the sake of the joy that was set before him endured the cross, disregarding its shame, and has taken his seat at the right hand of the throne of God."

First Peter 2:24 says, "He himself bore our sins in his body on the cross, so that, free from sins, we might live for righteousness; by his wounds you have been healed."

So the death of Jesus on the cross (his passion) and Jesus being raised from the dead (his resurrection) are central to the Christian faith. As I write in the introduction to *Spelunking Scripture: Easter*, "That Jesus died for our sins and was raised to new life by the power of God is the heart of the gospel."

CHAPTER 1

THE CONSPIRACY AGAINST JESUS
Matthew 26:1-5; Mark 14:1-2; Luke 22:1-2

> *It was two days before the Passover and the festival of Unleavened Bread. The chief priests and the scribes were looking for a way to arrest Jesus by stealth and kill him; for they said, "Not during the festival, or there may be a riot among the people." (Mark 14:1-2, NRSV)*

Matthew, Mark, and Luke are commonly known as the Synoptic Gospels. They are called "synoptic" because they see the story of Jesus from the same point of view. The chronology of the three Gospels is basically the same, and even some of the wording is the same. Most New Testament scholars believe that Mark was written first and that Matthew and Luke had access to Mark, then added additional material from their own sources.

Assuming that these passages in Matthew and Luke were based on the passage in Mark, it seems that Luke summarized Mark's account and explained that the festival of Unleavened Bread was called the Passover for those, like himself, who were not Jews. Any Jew would have known that the Festival of Unleavened Bread was called the Passover.

Matthew provides additional information in his passage. He begins with a "passion prediction" from Jesus that he would be handed over to be crucified. Matthew relates that the conspiracy took place in the palace of the high priest, who was called Caiaphas. Matthew quotes Mark directly in the words "to arrest Jesus by stealth and kill him" and "Not during the festival, or there may be a riot among the people."

Why did they want to kill Jesus? Maybe they had heard what the people were saying about him when he entered Jerusalem on Palm Sunday. According to Matthew, they said, "Hosanna to the Son of David!" (Matt 21:9). According to Mark, they said, "Blessed is the coming kingdom of our ancestor David!" (Mark 11:10). According to Luke, they said, "Blessed is the king who comes in the name of the Lord!" (Luke 19:38). The son of David, the coming kingdom, the king—no wonder the authorities felt threatened. Not to mention the idea that Jesus was the Messiah, the anointed one, the Christ.

A RIOT AMONG THE PEOPLE
Mark 14:1-2

It was a day we will never forget—January 6, 2021. I turned on the television and could hardly believe what I was seeing: a mob laying siege to the United States Capitol. Hundreds, maybe even thousands, of people rioted, shouting and carrying signs supporting then-President Donald Trump, who had been defeated in the recent 2020 election. Some broke windows, attacking and shoving past Capitol police officers and storming into the building.

It was the day Congress was scheduled to certify the election of Joe Biden as the next President of the United States, but the mob delayed that process. We learned that security personnel escorted members of Congress to secret safe havens to escape the potential violence against them. It was the closest we had ever seen in our lifetimes to insurrection against our government.

The Jewish leaders feared this would happen in Jerusalem should they publicly arrest Jesus. The chief priests and scribes feared there would be a "riot among the people," so they sought to arrest Jesus by stealth and have him killed.

It was just two days before Passover and the festival of Unleavened Bread. Pilgrims had come to the capital city, and Jesus was popular among many of them. As Luke puts it, "The chief priests and the scribes were looking for a way to put Jesus to death, for they were afraid of the people" (Luke 22:2). Matthew says, "the chief priests and the elders of the people gathered in the palace of the high priest, who was called Caiaphas, and they conspired to arrest Jesus by stealth and kill him" (Matt 26:3-4). So began the conspiracy against Jesus.

Opposition to Jesus really had begun long before that. Religious leaders had opposed Jesus since the beginning of his ministry. But things came to a head as the Passover festival approached and public support for Jesus became apparent. It happened on what we call "Palm Sunday," when crowds gathered to cheer Jesus as he entered Jerusalem on the back of a donkey. Matthew and Luke describe his subsequent cleansing of the temple, which further angered and alarmed the authorities. Luke summarizes the following days this way: "every day he was teaching in the temple…and all the people would get up early in the morning to listen to him…" (Luke 21:37-38).

It's easy to understand why the Jewish religious authorities were so concerned about Jesus. They saw him as a threat to their remaining in power. There were no democratic elections back then, but the will of the people might be expressed in other ways, such as a riot. What we saw in the United States on January 6, 2021, was an expression of that possibility. When their candidate lost the democratic election, some supporters of Donald Trump sought to keep him in power by rioting at the Capitol.

The conspiracy against Jesus began. According to their plans, Jesus would be kept from power not by a riot among the people but by the stealth of those in political power to have him arrested and killed. Jesus had predicted this would happen. He first predicted his passion in Matthew 16:13-23, Mark 8:27-33, and Luke 9:18-22. His second passion prediction is found in Matthew 17:22-23, Mark 9:30-32, and Luke 9:43b-45. There is a third passion prediction from Jesus in Matthew 20:17-19, Mark 10:32-34, and Luke 18:31-34. Then Matthew adds another at the beginning of the passage about the conspiracy against Jesus in Matthew 26:2. The conspiracy was no surprise, at least for Jesus. His disciples should have expected it too, but as Luke explained, "they understood nothing about all these things; in fact, what he said was hidden from them, and they did not grasp what was said" (Luke 18:34).

The passion predictions show that Jesus knew what was going on. He was not an unwitting victim of circumstance. When the conspiracy began against him, he did not run away and hide, nor did he marshal his followers to a popular uprising. Rather than trying to seize power through the riot of a mob, Jesus succumbed to power through his suffering on the cross. Jesus voluntarily gave himself for us. What amazing love!

In 1738 Charles Wesley expressed this amazing love in a hymn:

And can it be that I should gain
an interest in the Savior's blood?
Died He for me, who caused His pain?
For me, who Him to death pursued?
Amazing love! How can it be
that Thou, my God, shouldst die for me?
Amazing love! How can it be
that Thou, my God, shouldst die for me![1]

QUESTIONS FOR DISCUSSION/REFLECTION

1. How and why did Jesus predict his passion?
2. How and why was Jesus such a threat to the religious authorities?
3. Why was there not a riot among the people?
4. Why was it necessary for Jesus to voluntarily give himself for us?
5. What does the death of Jesus mean for you?

NOTE

[1] Charles Wesley, "And Can It Be, That I Should Gain?" 1738, https://hymnary.org/text/and_can_it_be_that_i_should_gain.

CHAPTER 2

THE ANOINTING AT BETHANY
Matthew 26:6-13; Mark 14:3-9 [Luke 7:36-50]

> *Now while Jesus was at Bethany in the house of Simon the leper, a woman came to him with an alabaster jar of very costly ointment, and she poured it on his head as he sat at the table. (Matthew 26:6-7, NRSV)*

Matthew and Mark tell one version of this story, with the setting in the home of Simon the leper. Luke tells another version in Luke 7:36-50, with the setting in a Pharisee's house. John tells yet another version in John 12:1-8, in the home of Lazarus, whom Jesus had raised from the dead. In all the versions, a woman anoints Jesus with costly ointment or perfume. In John's version, the woman is Mary, the sister of Martha and Lazarus. In Luke's version, the woman is identified as "a sinner." In Matthew and Mark, the woman is not identified. Since Luke's version of the story occurs earlier in his Gospel, it is not included in the Gospel parallels along with Matthew and Mark. Thus, Luke's version is not a part of the Passion Narrative since the anointing is placed much earlier in the story of Jesus.

IN REMEMBRANCE OF HER
Matthew 26:6-13

I am not an extravagant person. I drive an economy car. It's a newer model (because it's a lease), but it's small and fuel efficient and a Hyundai. No one would call it a luxury car. Linda and I have lived in the same house for nearly forty years. Most of the suits I wear on Sunday mornings (when I do wear a suit) are at least fifteen to twenty years old. Most of my golf equipment I bought used. I book my golf tee times online to get a better deal. When Linda and I travel, we use points from our credit card to pay for the plane tickets. I eat lunch at home almost every day to save on eating out. When we do eat out, we typically use coupons or gift cards someone has given us.

I'm not cheap, but I am frugal. We could not have put our two kids through college on a pastor's salary without being careful with our money. So you can't accuse me of being extravagant. That's why this story gets to me. The woman who poured the jar of expensive ointment over Jesus's head at the dinner party was wildly extravagant.

Matthew says it was just before Passover. Jesus had said to his disciples, "You know that after two days the Passover is coming, and the Son of Man will be handed over to be crucified" (Matt 26:2). The chief priests and the elders were already conspiring to arrest Jesus by stealth and kill him. But they had to be careful about doing it during the festival for fear of a riot among the people. This event (the anointing) happened behind the scenes when Jesus was in Bethany at the home of Simon the leper.

Apparently, this woman crashed the dinner party. She came with an alabaster jar of expensive perfume and poured it on Jesus's head as he sat at the table. When the disciples witnessed her extravagant gesture, they were angry at such a waste. John fills in details that Matthew does not give. John says Judas protested the loudest. Both John and Mark calculated that the ointment (or perfume) was worth 300 denarii, a huge sum, equal to a year's wage for a common worker. Judas said the ointment could have been sold and the money given to the poor. John adds that Judas said this not because he cared about the poor but because he was a thief. As treasurer for the group, Judas kept the common purse, and he stole from it (John 12:4-6).

There is a lot going on in this story. Jesus is having dinner in the home of Simon the leper. Judas is preparing to betray Jesus. The disciples are outraged at the waste of money that could have been given to the poor. But the woman gives Jesus the best that she has. Let's start with Judas and the disciples, who considered the woman's actions a waste.

I understand where they were coming from. I hate to waste money too. Although Judas had an ulterior motive in his protest, the ointment could have been sold and the money given to the poor. When Jesus defended the woman's actions, he was not discouraging the disciples from helping the poor. This story in Matthew 26 comes right after Matthew 25, where Jesus gave the disciples his famous parable about the sheep and the goats and "the least of these."

In the parable, the Son of Man comes in all his glory, surrounded by angels, and sits on the throne of judgment. All the nations of the earth are gathered before him. The Son of Man separates the people as a shepherd separates the sheep from the goats. They are judged not on the basis of who they are or what they believe but solely on the basis of what they have done. To those who will inherit the kingdom, the Son of Man says, "I was hungry and you gave me food, I was thirsty and you gave me something to drink, I was a stranger and you welcomed me, I was naked and you gave me clothing, I was sick and you took care of me, I was in prison and you visited me. Just as you did it to one of the least of these… you did it to me" (Matt 25:35-36, 40). The parable is about what Jesus expects us to do. Jesus expects his followers to take care of "the least of these." When Jesus said, "you always have the poor with you" (26:11), he wasn't saying we should be unconcerned about the poor. He was saying we will always have opportunities to care for the poor.

When I read again the parable of the sheep and the goats, it reminded me of the Warm Nights ministry conducted by our former church. One week each winter, our church took care of "the least of these." We provided food to the hungry, refreshment to the thirsty, welcome to strangers, clothing to those who needed it, care for those who were not well, and Christian compassion for those imprisoned by homelessness. We did it because what we do for the least of these, we do for Jesus. Words from the parable are inscribed on a plaque in the foyer over the doors to the church's sanctuary. The plaque is there to remind people every time they come to church that we have a responsibility to minister to the poor.

But the parable is about more than taking care of the poor. It is also about expressing our love and devotion to Jesus. That's what the woman was doing in Matthew 26. The jar of perfume was likely her most precious possession. It was worth a lot of money.

Personally, I don't own anything I could carry in my hands that is worth a year's wages. But I do have things of value. My time is valuable. My talents are valuable. And I have material possessions, including money, that are valuable.

Most of my material wealth is concentrated in various types of investments—our house, our bank accounts, our retirement accounts. There were no banks or brokerage firms in Jesus's time. The costly perfume may have been like the woman's retirement fund. It may have been her insurance for a rainy day. By pouring that expensive perfume on Jesus's head, the woman was giving Jesus the best she had. An old hymn begins, "Give of your best to the Master."[1] That's what she did—she gave her best to Jesus. It was a sacrificial gift, anticipating the sacrificial gift that Jesus would offer on the cross.

Did you notice the venue of that dinner with Jesus? It was an unlikely place, an unexpected place, in the home of Simon the leper. We don't know if Simon was a former leper whom Jesus had healed or if he still suffered from leprosy. Either way, it's almost shocking that Jesus would have dinner in Simon's home. Most people stayed away from lepers. Lepers were required by law to shout "unclean, unclean" wherever they came near other people. No one in his right mind would go near a leper's home, much less break bread with him, even if the leper had been healed. It was too great a risk. But Jesus was in the business of taking risks. His whole life was a risk. Jesus was the risk that God took to bring us to God's self.

We find Jesus dining in a most surprising place and receiving a most surprising gesture of generosity. Jesus recognized the woman's act was an act of love. It was also a prophetic act. She was symbolically anointing his body for burial. Anticipating his coming death on the cross, Jesus said what she had done was a beautiful thing. In that day, kings were also anointed. Jesus would be condemned and executed as the King of the Jews. He would be lifted upon a cross, but God would lift him up to become King of kings and Lord of lords.

It's ironic that Matthew never tells us the woman's name. It's ironic because henceforth, this story would be told in remembrance of her (v. 13). Yet Matthew doesn't even mention her name. John identifies the woman as Mary, the sister of Martha and Lazarus, and he places the anointing in the home of Lazarus, but Matthew leaves her anonymous. I think that's because Matthew wanted to focus more on the action than the person. He wanted to use her example of giving to inspire all of us to give of our best to Jesus.

The story is really about what God has done for us—what God has given us out of love. Jesus died on the cross for our sins. He took our punishment upon himself to make us whole and to set us free. We can do nothing to earn our salvation. It is a gift of grace. But we can do something in response to that great love. We can give of our best to the Master. We can give our time and our talents and our energies and, yes, our money in God's service.

I must admit I still feel the tension in this story. The needs of the world are so great. There are so many hurting people, so many hungry people, so many homeless people, that it does seem a waste not to sell the ointment and give the money to the poor. But we always have opportunities to do good. We will always have the poor with us. The Warm Nights ministry was a reminder of that. People without a home spent seven nights in our church building. God helped us to help them.

Food and shelter are necessary, but Jesus came to give us even greater things. He came to give us forgiveness. He came to give us salvation. He came to give us peace and hope. He came to give us love. He came to give us life in all its abundance, life that is eternal.

The woman who poured out the perfume performed a good service for Jesus. It was extravagant, yes, but sometimes extravagance is called for. After all, God was extravagant in God's love for us. What fragrant offering can we make in service to God?

QUESTIONS FOR DISCUSSION/REFLECTION

1. Why do you think the woman did what she did?
2. Why was it not a waste?
3. Have you ever given an extravagant gift?
4. What extravagant gift can you give to Jesus?
5. What do you think happened to the woman who anointed Jesus?

NOTE

[1] Howard B. Grose, "Give of Your Best to the Master," late 1800s, https://hymnary.org/text/give_of_your_best_to_the_master_give_of.

CHAPTER 3

JUDAS AGREES TO BETRAY JESUS
Matthew 26:14-16; Mark 14:10-11; Luke 22:3-6

Then one of the twelve, who was called Judas Iscariot, went to the chief priests and said, "What will you give me if I betray him to you?" They paid him thirty pieces of silver. (Matthew 26:14-15, NRSV)

Matthew says the chief priests paid Judas, one of Jesus's twelve disciples, thirty pieces of silver to betray his friend and teacher. Mark and Luke say they promised to give him money, but they don't give the amount. All three Gospels agree that Judas "began to look for an opportunity to betray him." At this point, Matthew and Mark do not give a motive for Judas's betrayal. Luke says that "Satan entered into Judas" (Luke 22:3). John says, "The devil had already put it into the heart of Judas son of Simon Iscariot to betray him" (John 13:2). John also says that Judas stole from the common purse (12:6). Why Judas sought to betray Jesus is perhaps multifaceted. Maybe more than greed was involved. Maybe Judas was disillusioned with Jesus. Or maybe Judas thought he could force Jesus's hand to take command. We do know that eventually Judas would regret what he had done.

THIRTY PIECES OF SILVER
Matthew 26:14-16

Karli is forty-three years old, but she is the developmental age of a first grader. She lives with her mother and stepfather in Rockville, Maryland, because she cannot live by herself. Karli is a grown woman chronologically, but she acts like a child. She collects dolls and Hello Kitty coloring books. She likes to wear pretty clothes, but she forgets to brush her teeth. She is easily led and manipulated. She doesn't recognize social cues or dangerous behaviors. She can only follow one instruction at a time. The tragedy is not who Karli is but that her condition could have been prevented. Karli is a victim of fetal alcohol syndrome. Her mother Kathy drank alcohol when she was pregnant with Karli. She says, "I adore my daughter. She's forever an innocent child. But not a day goes by that I don't ask myself, 'What if? What if alcohol hadn't been a part of my life?'"

Fetal alcohol spectrum disorder includes a range of impairments. It can cause impaired growth, intellectual disabilities, emotional and behavioral issues, vision problems, and speech and language delays. Tragically, the disabilities last a lifetime. There is no cure, though early intervention treatments can improve a child's development. It's not that Karli is a burden on her family. Kathy adds, "Karli is a blessing. She brings joy to everyone she knows." "But," Kathy admits, "it breaks my heart to think about why Karli is disabled."

Kathy started drinking alcohol when she was just a child. Her parents owned a restaurant in Olney, Maryland, that took on a nightclub atmosphere after the dinner hour. Because Kathy worked in the family business along with her siblings, she had access to alcohol. By the time Kathy turned twelve, she had become drunk more than once. She said, "Drinking made me feel grown up, cuter, smarter." At the age of fourteen, Kathy was the maid of honor at her sister's wedding. Kathy drank so many beers during the reception that she became intoxicated and fled the scene. She was in the early stages of alcoholism, experiencing periodic blackouts. In the tenth grade, Kathy got pregnant. She married the baby's father (a teenage boyfriend) and dropped out of school. Their son was born healthy, so Kathy didn't think her drinking was harmful. Soon she went back to work at the restaurant, waiting tables and tending bar. Nine months later, Kathy was pregnant again. Once again, she drank throughout her pregnancy.

A few months after Kathy turned eighteen, she gave birth to Karli. But Karli was not okay. Her problems became more apparent as she got older. At one point, Karli was diagnosed with cerebral palsy. But that proved to be a false diagnosis. Frankly, medical professionals didn't know what was wrong with her, except that she was falling farther and farther behind the other kids her age. Finally, when Karli was sixteen, Kathy took her to Georgetown University Hospital. After a battery of tests, the doctors concluded that Karli is a victim of fetal alcohol syndrome. Kathy says when the diagnosis was made, she thought she would die from the grief and guilt. Karli's condition was due to Kathy's behavior. Kathy had betrayed her daughter at the most fundamental level. She drank while she was pregnant, and her baby suffered irreversible consequences. The betrayal may not have been deliberate, but it was a betrayal nonetheless. After all, a mother's fundamental responsibility is to take care of her child.

In our scripture, Judas betrays Jesus. In the case of Judas, it was a deliberate betrayal. It was intentional. Judas knew exactly what he was doing. He went to the chief priests and asked them, "What will you give me if I betray him to you?" They paid Judas thirty pieces of silver. According to the book of Exodus, thirty pieces of silver was the price of a slave. If an ox gored a slave to death, the owner of the ox had to pay the owner of the slave thirty pieces of silver as a recompense

(Exod 21:32). So Judas sold Jesus for the price of a slave. "And from that moment on he began to look for an opportunity to betray him" (Matt 26:16).

Why did Judas do it, we wonder. Matthew doesn't say. Greed may have had something to do with it. John indicates that Judas was the treasurer of the disciples and kept the common purse. But maybe it was more complicated than money. Some have suggested that Judas was disillusioned. He finally figured out that Jesus was not the kind of Messiah Judas wanted him to be. Maybe Judas thought he could force Jesus's hand by betraying him to the authorities. Whatever his reason, John says the devil put it into Judas's heart to betray Jesus (John 13:2). In the end, betrayal is the work of the devil. Betrayal is a violation of trust. That's why the Bible is so unequivocal, for example, in its denunciation of adultery. Breaking marriage vows is a betrayal, a violation of trust. Cheating on a spouse causes great hurt and great harm.

Now, lest we demonize Judas, let us remember that all the disciples failed Jesus at some level. After Jesus was arrested that Thursday night in the Garden of Gethsemane, Matthew says, "all the disciples deserted him and fled" (26:56b). We also remember how Peter denied three times that he even knew Jesus (26:69-75). Yes, Jesus called Judas "the betrayer," but the rest of the twelve disciples betrayed him too.

To his credit, Judas did feel regret for what he had done. When Judas saw that Jesus had been condemned, Matthew says he "repented and brought back the thirty pieces of silver to the chief priests and the elders" (27:3). Judas said, "I have sinned by betraying innocent blood" (27:4). When the chief priests refused to take the money back, Judas threw down the thirty pieces of silver in the temple. Then, overwhelmed with remorse and guilt, Judas went and hanged himself.

In the end, Judas had a change of heart, but it was too late. He gave up in despair and took his own life. One wonders what would have happened had Judas not committed suicide. I have no doubt that Jesus would have forgiven him, just as Jesus forgave those who crucified him. After all, the death of Jesus was for the forgiveness of all our sins. But we must receive that forgiveness willingly for it to take effect. It is not forced on us. Peter received forgiveness and was restored to the fellowship, even after his three denials. The other disciples, even though they deserted Jesus, were restored to the fellowship and became leaders in the early church. Had Judas not given up and killed himself, perhaps he would have been restored too.

We tend to think of Judas as an evil person, and the devil did enter Judas for a time. But the devil didn't single him out because he was evil. The devil wants to enter all of us. All of us are subject to temptation. The devil even tried to tempt Jesus to betray God. After Jesus was baptized by John the Baptist, he spent forty days in the wilderness being tempted by the devil (Matt 4). And in the Garden of Gethsemane, Jesus resisted the temptation to avoid the cross (Matt 26:36-42). Three times he prayed that the cup of suffering might pass from him. The book of Hebrews says Jesus was tempted in every way that we are, yet he was without sin (Heb 4:15). Jesus understands our failings and is able to sympathize with our weaknesses.

The British actor Jeremy Irons has played a lot of villains during his movie career. Jeremy says he enjoys playing villains because in many situations it's difficult to know who the villains are and who the good guys are. "People tend to think in black and white," he says, "and of course, we are all gray."[1] That could make a title for a sermon: "We Are All Gray." Nobody is all good or all bad. We are all mixtures of the good and the bad. But Jesus came to forgive the bad in us and to make us good. We have all betrayed Jesus in one way or another, but betrayal does not have to be the final word. The final word is forgiveness. The final word is redemption. The final word is grace.

A popular song from the movie *Frozen* could be the theme song for every Christian. The song is "Let It Go." The lyrics have a powerful message: "The past is in the past! …Let it go!"[2]

We've all made mistakes. We've all sinned and fallen short of the glory of God. We've all betrayed Jesus in some way or another, intentionally or unintentionally. The good news of the gospel is we can let it go. Jesus died on the cross to forgive us of our sins. Jesus was raised from the grave to give us new life in him. Let it go.

Kathy has learned to "let it go." Rather than remaining in her self-hatred and self-blame over what her drinking did to her daughter, Kathy has made it her mission in life to tell the story so that others might not make the same mistakes. Kathy says she is trying to do everything in her power to prevent this from happening to another child.

Today Kathy Mitchell is vice president of the National Organization on Fetal Alcohol Syndrome. It's a nonprofit that educates on the risks of alcohol use during pregnancy. Kathy hopes that going public with her story will help destigmatize the issue, prevent other young mothers from doing what she did, and prevent other children from becoming victims of fetal alcohol syndrome.[3]

According to the American Academy of Pediatrics, there is no known safe level of alcohol consumption during any trimester of pregnancy. Yet, according to the Centers of Disease Control, at least one in ten pregnant women acknowledge drinking alcohol. Kathy is trying to help those women realize it is a risk they should not take. Her guilt and remorse are painful, but that's not what preoccupies her today. Her life is preoccupied with helping her daughter Karli become all that she can be and with helping other mothers take care of their babies too. Rather than being consumed by regret, Kathy has learned to "let it go."

Now, every day she strives to make a positive difference in the life of her daughter and in the lives of other sons and daughters yet to be born.

Every life is precious, more precious than even thirty pieces of silver. Jesus died on the cross because every life is precious. Jesus died so that even betrayers might be forgiven. We are all flawed and broken, but Jesus died and rose again to make us whole and new. The past is past—let it go. The author of Hebrews said, "let us also lay aside every weight and the sin that clings so closely, and let us run with perseverance the race that is set before us, looking to Jesus the pioneer and perfecter of our faith, who for the sake of the joy that was set before him endured the cross, disregarding its shame, and has taken his seat at the right hand of the throne of God" (Heb 12:1-2).

All have sinned, but Jesus has saved us and given us new life. Let it go.

QUESTIONS FOR DISCUSSION/REFLECTION

1. Why do you think Judas betrayed Jesus?
2. Why do you think Peter and the other disciples behaved as they did?
3. Can you think of ways that you have betrayed Jesus?
4. Why did Judas kill himself?
5. What is the power of forgiveness?

NOTES

[1] AARP *The Magazine*, February/March 2016, p. 13.

[2] Kristen Anderson-Lopez and Robert Lopez, "Let It Go," Wonderland Music Company, January 2014.

[3] Alexandra Rockey Fleming, "A life undone by her mother's drinking," *The Washington Post*, January 19, 2016, E1, E6.

CHAPTER 4

PREPARATION FOR THE PASSOVER
Matthew 26:17-19; Mark 14:12-16; Luke 22:7-13

> *Then came the day of Unleavened Bread, on which the Passover lamb had to be sacrificed. So Jesus sent Peter and John, saying, "Go and prepare the Passover meal for us that we may eat it." (Luke 22:7-8, NRSV)*

Matthew gives an abbreviated version of the preparation for the Passover meal. Mark and Luke provide more details, such as who would secure a place for the meal (Luke tells us it was Peter and John; Mark simply says it was two of the disciples) and how they would identify the owner of the house who would host the Passover supper.

The background for the customary observance of the Passover is found in Exodus 12:14-20 and Deuteronomy 16:5-8. Mark and Luke do not state the identity of the homeowner except that he would be a man carrying a jar of water. Since carrying a jar of water was normally a woman's work, Peter and John would readily recognize the homeowner for his unusual behavior. Securing a place not previously associated with Jesus probably allowed them to meet in a secure location unknown to Jesus's enemies.

MAKING A PLACE FOR JESUS
Luke 22:7-13

The movie *The Great Debaters* is based on the true story of the Wiley College debate team.[1] Wiley College is a small African American liberal arts school in Marshall, Texas. During the 1930s the Wiley College debate teams were among the best in the nation. But the success of the debate program was little known because Black colleges were not allowed to compete with predominantly white schools. Even debating other African American colleges was not easy. In the days of Jim Crow and the Ku Klux Klan, African Americans suffered daily indignities, abuses, and threats. Travel was difficult, for most hotels and boarding houses closed their doors to African Americans. When the debate team from Wiley College traveled to other schools, they had to seek lodging in private homes of sympathetic hosts. Those were the days of legal and institutional racial segregation when African Americans risked their lives if they dared to cross racial boundaries.

In a gripping episode in the movie, the debate team is traveling by car through the rural countryside at night. They happen unexpectedly upon the aftermath of a lynching. A Black man has been hanged by a noose and set on fire, with a racist mob gathered around. The debate coach, an English professor at the college, tells his team members not to look, but they cannot help but see the smoldering body dangling from the tree. They speed away in shock and horror, but none of them is able to sleep that night in the home where they are staying. They realize that they are in hostile territory as they seek haven from the hatred.

It was like that for Jesus and his disciples when they came to Jerusalem for the Passover. They were in hostile territory, and they sought haven from the hatred. Luke 22 begins with this chilling portent: "Now the festival of Unleavened Bread, which is called the Passover, was near. The chief priests and the scribes were looking for a way to put Jesus to death" (vv. 1-2). Jesus knew that they were looking for a way to kill him. He had predicted to his disciples that he would be handed over to be crucified. Some of his disciples had tried to dissuade him from coming to Jerusalem. But Jesus had set his face toward the city, for above all, he must do the Father's will.

Still, this was a suicide mission. If there were a way to do the Father's will without drinking the bitter cup of suffering, Jesus prayed for that (see Matt 26:36-44). Besides, his work was not yet finished. He wanted to share the Passover one last time with his disciples. He needed to use that final Passover to explain what his coming death would mean. So it was necessary to find a place to observe the Passover where they would be safe from the hatred of the chief priests and scribes. That explains the unusual procedure that Jesus prescribed to Peter and John for preparing the Passover meal.

They were to go into the city and meet a man carrying a jar of water. That was a sign. Typically, women carried the water. It was a clandestine rendezvous. The man carrying the jar of water would lead them to a house. There they were to ask the owner of the house about the guest room for Jesus and his disciples. The owner would show them a large upstairs room, furnished for the meal. They would prepare for Passover there.

If this sounds rather mysterious, it is because Jesus and his disciples needed a place out of the public eye to share the Passover. Remember that Jesus and most of his disciples were Galileans. Jerusalem was not their home. They were only visitors, along with the throngs of other Passover pilgrims who had come to the city for the holy festival. They needed a place to celebrate Passover, but they needed a secret place. If their whereabouts became known, the authorities might come to arrest Jesus before the Passover.

It was necessary for Jesus to share the Passover with his disciples one last time, for in the context of the Seder supper Jesus explained the meaning of his coming death. During the Last Supper, Jesus took the bread and the cup and instituted the Lord's Supper. The bread and cup were symbolic of his body and blood. The unleavened bread and the wine represented his coming death that would be a sacrifice for the forgiveness of sins. Jesus would give his life so that all who believed in him might receive life. His coming death would mean salvation for all who had faith in him.

That is why they needed a special place to observe Passover. The chief priests and the scribes were already conspiring to kill Jesus. They sought the opportunity to seize him in secret to avoid a public outcry. The Passover meal would have been a perfect setting for that. But Jesus was not ready to be seized and arrested. He needed to explain to his disciples what his suffering and death would mean. So they found a private place, a secret place, an upper room known only to the disciples and the owner of the house, to share that last Passover meal.

It may be that Jesus had made prior arrangements with the homeowner. Maybe the owner of the house was a secret disciple of Jesus. After all, it was risky for this unnamed person to allow Jesus and his disciples to meet there. He could have been accused of harboring a criminal, charged with being a co-conspirator with Jesus, and subject to arrest himself. It was brave for this homeowner to allow Jesus and his disciples to meet in the upper room to share the Passover.

Apparently this upper room became the meeting place for the disciples in Jerusalem after the crucifixion, which supports the possibility that the homeowner was a secret disciple of Jesus. In John's Gospel, two times after the resurrection, Jesus appeared to his disciples in a house in Jerusalem. In the book of Acts, after the resurrected Jesus had ascended into heaven, the followers of Jesus went back into the city and entered an upstairs room where they were staying. Perhaps this was the same place where they shared the Last Supper and the Lord's Supper with Jesus. It became a kind of unofficial base of operations for the disciples after Jesus left them. This upper room in Jerusalem may have become the first meeting place of the early church. Surely the owner of the house with the upper room was a follower of Jesus.

There is another intriguing clue to the identity of the homeowner. Sometime later, as we read in Acts 12, King Herod "laid violent hands" on some members of the church (v. 1). James, the brother of John, was killed, and Peter was arrested and thrown into prison, likely to receive the same fate. But during the night, before Herod could bring him out for execution, an angel of the Lord opened the prison door, released Peter from his shackles, and set him free. Upon his release from prison, Peter went to the place where the church was meeting and praying for him. The meeting place was the home of Mary, the mother of John Mark.

Many church members had gathered there to pray. Could this have been the house with the upper room? If so, that would mean the owner of the house who offered Jesus and his disciples the upper room for the Passover was John Mark's father. This same John Mark later wrote the Gospel of Mark, probably the first written account of the life of Jesus.

We know from the writings of Paul that Mark eventually became one of his most trusted associates and an early leader of the church. Mark's mother was certainly a follower of Jesus, and it may be that his father was an early follower too. This is another tantalizing clue: In Mark's Gospel, and only in Mark's Gospel (14:51-52), we are told that after Jesus was arrested in the Garden of Gethsemane, an unnamed young man also was seized. He wore nothing more than a linen cloth, a bedsheet, perhaps. The authorities grabbed hold of the cloth, but the young man managed to wriggle free and ran away naked. Could this have been Mark? Maybe he was asleep downstairs in his parents' home while Jesus and the disciples met upstairs in the upper room. Maybe he awoke from his sleep and followed Jesus and the others to the Garden of Gethsemane, wrapped only in a bedsheet. Maybe Mark is the one who ran away naked after Jesus was arrested. If so, the house with the upper room may have been Mark's family home.

Of course, this is speculation. We do not know for certain the identity of the owner of the house with the upper room. All we know is that the owner provided a place for Jesus and the disciples to share the Passover. He did this one thing and was not heard from again. Like many of the other ordinary people of the Passion, he appeared in the story only briefly and then disappeared from view. We do not know his name, but we remember what he did. He made a place for Jesus. He provided Jesus a haven from the hatred. His home became a welcoming place in hostile territory where Jesus could gather one last time with his friends and say goodbye before the cross. Even if the owner of the house were the father of Mark, we don't remember his name, but we remember his courage and his hospitality and his love. He made a place for Jesus, and isn't that what all of us are called to do?

The reason we remember such ordinary people of the Passion is because all of us are ordinary people too. Yet even though we are all ordinary people, we still can do something for Jesus. Simon the leper gave a dinner party for Jesus. An unnamed woman broke open an alabaster jar of expensive perfume and poured it on Jesus's head, anointing his body beforehand for burial. An unnamed owner of a house with an upper room in Jerusalem provided a place for Jesus to share the Last Supper with his disciples. Those ordinary people all did what they could for Jesus.

That is what we are called to do as well: to do what we can for Jesus by the way we live. We are all ordinary people, but we can make a place for Jesus too—a place in our lives and a place in our hearts. We who believe in Jesus are the church, the body of Christ. The Spirit of Christ continues to dwell in the ordinary people like us.

QUESTIONS FOR DISCUSSION/REFLECTION

1. Why do you think Jesus gathered with his disciples in an upper room?
2. What do you think about the owner of the house with the upper room?
3. Can you think of other ways that ordinary people served Jesus?
4. What space can you offer Jesus?
5. How can you make a place for Jesus in your life?

NOTE

[1] *The Great Debaters*, dir. Denzel Washington, Weinstein Company and Metro-Goldwyn-Mayer, 2007.

CHAPTER 5

THE TRAITOR
Matthew 26:20-25; Mark 14:17-21; Luke 22:14, 21-23

> *When it was evening, he took his place with the twelve; and while they were eating, he said, "Truly I tell you, one of you will betray me." (Matthew 26:21-22, NRSV)*

The betrayal was no surprise to Jesus. At the Last Supper Jesus told his disciples that one of them would betray him. Of the three Synoptic Gospels, only Matthew includes the response of Judas: "Surely not I, Rabbi?" (Matt 26:25). It's as if Matthew wants the reader to see that Jesus had Judas in mind when he said, "one of you will betray me." All the disciples were distressed, but only Judas knew who Jesus was talking about. All the disciples would run out on Jesus, and Peter would deny him, but it was Judas who would betray him.

THIS IS MY BODY, THIS IS MY BLOOD
Matthew 26:20-29

Ali was born in Louisville, Kentucky, to a mother who suffered from paranoid schizophrenia. For the first six years of her life, Ali and her mother drifted in and out of homelessness. Although Ali loved her mother, it was no way to live. When Ali was six years old, she was placed into foster care by Child Protective Services. A short time after that, Ali's mother gave birth to Ali's younger sister. The two of them were able to spend some time with their mother off and on for the next few years, but their mother was still not well. Ali saw her mother for the last time at age ten, during a volatile supervised home visit. After that, a judge ruled that the mother's parental rights be terminated for the safety of the children and that the girls be put up for adoption.

When Ali turned twelve, she and her sister were adopted. The two girls moved to Ft. Hood, Texas, with a military couple who were their new parents. But things did not go well. After her adoptive father was deployed to Iraq, the relationship between Ali and her adoptive mother began to deteriorate. While in foster care, Ali had developed a habit of hoarding food, probably because she was worried about having enough to eat. The adoptive mother suffered from anorexia and placed restrictions on the girls about food. Afraid of going hungry, Ali began to steal food from her own home.

Her adoptive mother grounded Ali for stealing food and banned her from the kitchen. Ali wasn't allowed to go downstairs by herself anymore. The adoptive mother put a buzzer on Ali's door so she would know if Ali left her room. The adoptive mother took Ali and her sister out of school so she could exercise full control over their lives. Ali responded by running away from home. Eventually, her adoptive parents gave up on her. Ali was moved into the Methodist Children's Home in Waco, Texas, a residential facility that provided schooling and other support. Ironically, instead of hating living at the Methodist Children's Home, Ali loved it. Although her adoptive parents had exposed her to God, it was only at the children's home that Ali began to find her own faith.

Looking back, Ali says, "There's no reason I should have survived and then gone on to be functional. It's only my complete dependence on Jesus that makes anything good." With support from a staff member at the children's home, Ali was able to grieve for her family and her devastating experiences of growing up. While finishing high school at the children's home in Waco, Ali began to dream about attending Baylor University after she graduated. She figured it was an impossible dream because of her lack of finances. But the university awarded her a scholarship, and Ali moved five minutes from the Methodist Children's Home in Waco to a dorm at Baylor.

Ali said, "To be honest, coming into Baylor, I thought I'd drop out the first year. Living in trauma, you don't think past the next day. I had no idea what I was doing, and I was alone, absolutely alone." But Ali would not be alone for long. During her freshman year at Baylor, friends invited Ali to attend a church in Waco.

It was a part of the deep healing Ali began to experience during her freshman year. The healing included beginning the process of forgiving her adoptive mother, with whom she had cut ties after entering college. This was made more difficult because the family had moved, and they didn't tell her.

During her sophomore year, Ali felt that God was releasing her from a relationship with her adoptive parents. They had not communicated with her in months, but she still felt burdened that she should try to have a relationship with them. When Ali began to feel that God was releasing her from that obligation, she felt like a burden was lifted. She felt free from something that she thought she would carry for the rest of her life. Although still alone, she began to feel liberated, set free.

Just a few days after Ali felt that the Lord released her from her adoptive parents, a family in her church took her out to lunch. The family included Katie, one of Ali's best friends at Baylor, and her parents Cindy and Joe. Cindy was a senior lecturer in the School of Engineering and Computer Science at Baylor. Over lunch, Cindy told Ali that she and her husband wanted to adopt her. Ali was in shock. Her first reaction was, "No, I've been there, done that." But then she began to consider the radical offer. She started to feel in her spirit, "This is the Lord." On December 16, 2011, Ali was adopted for the second time.

Although adult adoptions are not as complicated as minor adoptions, there were still plenty of challenges. Because Ali was busy with her studies, it was tough to find the time to talk to her new family and get to know them on a deeper level. It was a learning experience. Ali had to learn to trust again. But they worked at it together, and Ali became a part of the family. Cindy said, "It's powerful to realize what God can do with anyone's circumstances and use them for good. You can so clearly see the hand of the Lord on her life."[1]

In our scripture, Jesus gathers with his disciples in an upper room to share the Passover. He knew that it would be their Last Supper together. While they ate, Jesus said, "one of you will betray me." It must have been incredibly difficult for Jesus to break bread with his traitor. Each disciple asked him with great distress, "Surely not I, Lord?" Then Judas, who had betrayed him for thirty pieces of silver, disingenuously said, "Surely not I, Rabbi?" Jesus replied, "You have said so."

While they were eating, Jesus took a loaf of bread, and after blessing it he broke it and gave it to the disciples. "Take, eat," he said. "This is my body." He did the same with a cup after giving thanks. "Drink from it, all of you," he said, "for this is my blood of the covenant, which is poured out for many for the forgiveness of sins."[2]

My guess is that at the time, the disciples had no idea what Jesus was talking about. The bread and the cup were elements of the Passover supper they had just shared together. But this talk about his body and his blood must have mystified them. How could they have understood it then?

Only after Jesus died on the cross did they begin to grasp the symbolism. His body and his blood were the sacrifice for their sins. Jesus was giving himself for them out of love.

For three years the disciples had been with Jesus. They had heard him teach and seen him heal. They had witnessed his confrontations with the religious authorities and his acts of compassion toward the lowly and the downtrodden. They had been invited to share the most personal moments with Jesus. Yet still they did not understand all that Jesus had for them. He wanted to be more than their friend and their Lord; he wanted to welcome them into the family of God. Jesus used the bread and the cup as symbols of his own flesh and blood. He was inviting the disciples to become his family, to become his flesh and blood, through his sacrifice on the cross.

The apostle Paul understood this when he spoke of our adoption into the family of God. In Galatians 4:4-5 Paul wrote, "But when the fullness of time had come, God sent his Son, born of a woman, born under the law…so that we might receive adoption as children." In Ephesians 1:5 Paul wrote, "He destined us for adoption as his children through Jesus Christ." That's what the bread and the cup are about; that's what the Lord's Supper is about. It's about what God has done through Jesus to adopt us into God's family. It's about what God has done through Christ to overcome our aloneness and to bring us home to God's self.

Jesus said of the bread, "this is my body." But when we receive Jesus into our hearts, we become the body of Christ. We become the family of God.

When Cindy told Ali that the family wanted to adopt her, she could hardly believe it. She had felt so alone, and now they wanted to welcome her into their family. So Ali became a part of two families. She became a part of Cindy's family, and she became a part of God's family. Ali credits God with the radical healing, transformation, and liberation that has occurred in her life.

That's what Jesus came to do for all of us—to heal the broken places in our lives, transform us into his image, and set us free. That's what the bread and the cup of Communion represent—what God has done through Jesus to welcome us into God's family.

We are the body of Christ and individually members of him (1 Cor 12:27). We who believe in Jesus have been adopted, born again, and welcomed into God's family. Every time you take and eat, and every time you take and drink, remember there is a place at the table for you.

QUESTIONS FOR DISCUSSION/REFLECTION

1. Why did Jesus say, "one of you will betray me"?
2. What was Jesus's attitude toward Judas?
3. Have you ever felt betrayed?
4. Have you ever betrayed Jesus?
5. How has Jesus made a plan to welcome all of us into God's family?

NOTES

[1] Ali's story is told in "Vessel: Baylor Student's Life Takes Shape in Unexpected Ways," *Baylor Lariat*, May 4, 2015, https://baylorlariat.com/2015/05/04/vessel-baylor-students-life-takes-shape-in-unexpected-ways/.

[2] We will discuss the Lord's Supper as a thanksgiving meal in chapter 6.

CHAPTER 6

THE INSTITUTION OF THE LORD'S SUPPER
Matthew 26:26-29; Mark 14:22-25; Luke 22:15-20

Then he took a loaf of bread, and when he had given thanks, he broke it and gave it to them, saying, "This is my body, which is given for you. Do this in remembrance of me." (Luke 22:19, NRSV)

We call it the "Lord's Supper," "Communion," or the "Eucharist," but it was more of a symbolic ritual than a meal. The bread and the cup of wine were symbols of Jesus's body and blood. Jesus used the traditional Passover meal to interpret what his coming death on the cross would mean—a sacrifice for the forgiveness of our sins. The elements of bread and wine were not uncommon, but Jesus gave them a meaning that made those common elements holy. Henceforth, whenever his followers partook of the bread and the cup, they did it in remembrance of Jesus.

THANKSGIVING FEAST
Matthew 26:26-29

Thanksgiving is a big deal here in America. Almost everyone celebrates Thanksgiving, whether they are religious or not. For most families, Thanksgiving involves a big meal. Many families serve turkey and dressing, pumpkin pie, and other traditional foods for Thanksgiving. But the origin of the holiday goes beyond food for a meal.

Perhaps you remember the story of the first Thanksgiving in America. It was celebrated by the Pilgrims in 1621 in what is now Plymouth, Massachusetts. They had arrived in the New World the year before, in 1620, after a harrowing trip across the Atlantic Ocean aboard the *Mayflower*.

They left England to escape religious persecution, but the voyage was more arduous than they expected, and the conditions in the New World were more severe than they ever imagined. After 65 days on the ocean, the 102 seasick souls were weary and weather beaten. They had intended to land much farther south, but the seas were too rough and the *Mayflower* too fragile to go on.

Their first winter in New England was unmerciful. Cold, hunger, and disease took a terrible toll. Of the 102 settlers who arrived on the *Mayflower*, 42 died during the first year. Yet, one year later, Governor William Bradford declared a day of prayer and thanksgiving.

With so much hardship and suffering and death, you might wonder what those Pilgrims had to be thankful for. But they did give thanks. They spent three days feasting and praying, and they invited some Native American neighbors to join them in their thanksgiving. Together, 90 members of the Wampanoag people along with survivors of the *Mayflower* celebrated the first Thanksgiving in America. That was a notable and exceptional event, given the way that many Native Americans have been treated throughout most of American history. But the Pilgrims welcomed their neighbors and gave thanks, not for the hardships but for the love of God that had sustained them.[1]

The people in the Bible did not necessarily celebrate the fourth Thursday of November as Thanksgiving Day, but they gathered as family and friends to share a meal. Perhaps the most important occasion for such a celebration was Passover, when families and friends would come together to share the Seder or Passover feast.

For Jews, the Seder commemorated the exodus of their ancestors from bondage in Egypt. It was a "thanksgiving" meal to remember a particular event in their history. For Jews even today, it is still a sacred celebration. In the United States, the American Thanksgiving is more generic. Sometimes we remember the thanksgiving feast in Plymouth Colony shared by the pilgrims with their indigenous neighbors after their first hard year in the New World. But mainly it's about food and family and friends.

Just as Thanksgiving is a communal celebration for people in the United States today, the Passover was a communal celebration for Jews in the Bible. Nobody celebrated Passover alone. Typically, a group of twelve or more family members or friends came together to celebrate. Because the Seder meal usually included lamb as well as other foods symbolic of Passover, it didn't make sense to slaughter a lamb for only a few people. So, when it came time for Jesus to celebrate the Passover, he naturally wanted to share this meal with his disciples. That meant at least thirteen of them were gathered around the Passover table. Others may have attended the celebration in the upper room, but we know for sure that the group included Jesus and the twelve disciples.

After they ate what would be their "last supper" together, Jesus introduced a new thanksgiving tradition. He took some unleavened bread left over from the Seder meal. He blessed it and broke it, then gave it to his disciples and said, "Take, eat; this is my body" (v. 26). It is unlikely that the disciples fully understood what that meant, but they took and ate the bread. Then Jesus took a cup of wine, also left over from the Seder meal. Jesus said, "Drink from it, all of you, for this is my blood of the covenant, which is poured out for many for the forgiveness of sins" (v. 28). Again, it is unlikely that the disciples fully understood, but they passed the cup among them and drank from it.

This was the night Jesus was betrayed (see chapter 5, "The Traitor"), the night before he died. Only in retrospect would the disciples come to understand that the bread and the cup were symbols of Jesus's body and blood. Only in retrospect would they understand that "the Lord's Supper" was symbolic of the sacrifice Jesus would make on the cross. But soon after that, and even to this day, every time the followers of Jesus eat the bread and drink from the cup, they do it in remembrance of him.

In a sense, every time we eat the bread and drink from the cup, we share a thanksgiving meal. There's no turkey or dressing, no potatoes or pumpkin pie. There's only the bread and the cup—often small bits of bread and tiny plastic cups. But the symbolism of this thanksgiving meal is at the very heart of our faith. We believe that Jesus gave his body and shed his blood for the forgiveness of our sins. What better reason to give thanks?

We call this observance Communion or the Lord's Supper. Some of our Christian friends call it the Eucharist. That word comes from the Greek word that means "to give thanks." When we remember what Jesus has done for us, how can we not give thanks?

Every time we come to the Communion table, the feast is spread before us, and our host, the risen Christ, is with us. So we take the bread and eat, and we take the cup and drink, and above all, we give thanks.

QUESTIONS FOR DISCUSSION/REFLECTION

1. Why did Jesus want to share Passover with his disciples?
2. What meaning did Jesus give to the bread and the cup?
3. In what sense is the Lord's Supper a thanksgiving meal?
4. Who is invited to share the Lord's Supper?
5. How has Communion divided Christians instead of uniting them?

NOTE

[1] History.com Editors, "Thanksgiving 2024," *History*, January 31, 2024, https://www.history.com/topics/thanksgiving/history-of-thanksgiving#.

CHAPTER 7

PETER'S DENIAL PREDICTED
Matthew 26:30-35; Mark 14:26-31; Luke 22:31-34, 39+

> *Peter said to him, "Even though all become deserters, I will not." Jesus said to him, "Truly I tell you, this day, this very night, before the cock crows twice, you will deny me three times." (Mark 14:29-30, NRSV)*

According to Matthew and Mark, after the disciples went with Jesus to the Mount of Olives, he said to them, "You will all become deserters." Peter took exception and vowed not to desert Jesus. After Jesus predicted that Peter would deny him three times before the cock crowed twice, Peter vowed to stay with Jesus, even if he should die with him. The other disciples vowed the same. In Luke 22:33, Peter declares, "Lord, I am ready to go with you to prison and to death!" Thus, in all three Synoptic Gospels, Peter promises to remain faithful to Jesus. And in all three Synoptic Gospels, Jesus predicts Peter's three denials.

THE POINTER
Mark 14:26-31

More than a hundred years ago, a church in Ohio had a duly elected officer called "the Pointer." It was the duty of this church official to stand every Sunday morning in the pulpit alongside the preacher. During the sermon, the Pointer did exactly what his title implied—he pointed. He picked out particular people in the congregation and pointed at them. Whenever the preacher made a strong statement condemning this sin or scoffing at that transgression, the Pointer made sure the message was directed to the appropriate individuals. "You there," the Pointer would cry, "pay attention! This applies to you."

I don't know of any churches that have "pointers" around today. Most preachers can do pretty well on their own.

The pastor of a church in Alabama was asked to speak to a preschool class in Vacation Bible School. After the teacher introduced him as the pastor of the church, he asked the children if any of them knew what the word "pastor" means.

One little girl answered, "Doesn't that mean to bother somebody?" The teacher spoke up, "No, he said 'pastor,' not 'pester.'"

The little girl's confusion is understandable. Whether we use a pointer or not, some pastors do pester people from the pulpit. I try not to preach overly negative messages, but I do recognize that from time to time what I say in a sermon might bother someone. My goal is not for people to leave church with a load of guilt, weighed down with worry about their sins and transgressions. My goal is just the opposite: I want people to leave church renewed, refreshed, revived, and relieved of undue worry. But the truth is, if our lives were already perfect, we would not need sermons.

So part of worship is getting pestered. We don't use a "pointer" to indicate individual sins. But most preachers will step on a few toes from time to time. I don't like to do that. I don't like to make people mad or feel guilty. In fact, I feel guilty when I make others feel guilty. But this happens from time to time because all of us need to have our toes stepped on. I include myself at the head of that list.

Someone has noticed that whenever you point a finger at anyone, you have at least three fingers pointed back at yourself. A preacher must always be willing to admit that he or she is among all sinners. The preacher who thinks he or she is better than everyone else is guilty of pride, hypocrisy, deception, and probably a lot more.

In the text from Mark's Gospel, there is plenty of blame to go around. The disciples let Jesus down in his hour of greatest need. Every single disciple failed Jesus in some way. One of the twelve, Judas, betrayed him for thirty pieces of silver. The disciples closest to Jesus—Peter, James, and John—fell asleep when Jesus needed them most. Later, Peter denied three times that he even knew Jesus. Finally, all the disciples ran away. After Jesus was arrested, they hid out like scared rabbits. They deserted Jesus when his life was on the line. If we want a picture of failure and sin, we should look no further than what the disciples did on the night before Jesus died.

We don't talk about failure and sin all that much. Some churches still feature plenty of pulpit pounding with loud and long sermons, but these days most people don't want that and won't stand for it (or sit for it). Most people I know will not tolerate having a preacher scream at them and tell them how bad they are. I don't like that either.

But just because we don't want to hear sermons about sin doesn't mean sin has disappeared. Just because we don't get lambasted every week in church doesn't mean we are blameless. Preaching styles have changed, but the human heart has not. Sin and failure and guilt are still with us. The disciples who failed Jesus are not so far removed from us.

Most of us, at some level, deal with our own mistakes and failures and guilt. As a minister, I have dealt with a certain amount of guilt over my professional failings. My first few years out of seminary, I felt guilty about taking a day off because I believed that taking time away from ministerial duties meant giving less than my best. It's easy for pastors to feel that our work is never done. I often worked sixty- to seventy-hour weeks.

I eventually learned that working like that is unrealistic. Someone has called it the "walk-on-water syndrome," the idea that ministers must be superhuman. I now recognize that taking a day off is necessary for effective ministry. Still, some feelings of guilt continue. I feel tremendous guilt whenever someone drops out of church, for whatever reason. Even if it wasn't my fault, I feel a sense of personal failure.

My guess is that most people, whatever their life's work, experience feelings of failure. We tend to set incredibly high standards for ourselves, and then we fail to measure up. We lose patience with people we have to work with, or we don't complete a project on time, or we miscalculate consequences, or we make errors in judgment. Our work can be the source of much failure and guilt.

Or we can feel like failures in our relationships. Almost every parent I know feels guilty about mistakes they have made in raising their children. When I consider my own shortcomings as a parent, I breathe a sigh of relief that my kids have turned out as well as they have. Being a parent is almost guaranteed to make you feel like a failure, at least once in a while.

So is being a husband or a wife. Marriage is difficult. In a time of anger or frustration or boredom, we say things to our spouses we don't really mean. We get so wrapped up in our own issues that we fail to see the needs of our marriage partners. We take each other for granted, or we use each other as dumping grounds for our own problems. We place unrealistic expectations on each other, and then we judge each other too critically. All meaningful relationships entail the risk of failure.

Then, there is our religious life, our commitment to Christ. There is plenty of room for failure. Who among us always turns the other cheek, always goes the second mile, always is ready to forgive, always loves our neighbors as we love ourselves? Who among us is always kind and compassionate and nonjudgmental and generous and unselfish? Who among us never lets Jesus down? We were not there that night when the disciples ran out on Jesus, but we run out on him in our own ways. Time and again, we are only half-hearted in our commitment, more concerned with saving our own skins than following Jesus along the difficult road of self-sacrifice.

How do we deal with our shortcomings and weaknesses and imperfections? We can learn from what happened on Jesus's last night. Notice two things.

First, Jesus was not shocked by the disciples' failure. Disappointed, yes. Hurt, yes. But shocked, no. He saw it coming. He predicted they would all fall away. Even when they protested, even when they pledged their undying devotion, Jesus recognized their imperfect faith. He knew them better than they knew themselves. And Jesus knows us better than we know ourselves. Jesus is not shocked when we mess up. Disappointed, yes. Hurt, yes. But not shocked, not appalled, not repulsed. If we were perfect, we would have no need for a Savior. If we were without sin, there would have been no need for a cross.

What does this mean? Does this mean our sin doesn't matter? Of course, it matters. Sin always carries consequences. Sin always causes hurt. But Jesus accepts our humanness, and we can accept our humanness too. We can learn to admit our mistakes and acknowledge that we all have some distance to go in our growth and maturity. Occasionally, we can even laugh at ourselves; we can learn not to take ourselves so seriously that every mistake drives us to self-destruction. We can accept our humanity because Jesus accepts us the way we are.

Notice something else. Jesus not only predicted the disciples' failure but also predicted their redemption. Jesus accepted the disciples for who they were, but he also saw in them something better than they were: he saw in them something of what they could become. Jesus saw that their failure did not have to be the final word.

Jesus said, "after I am raised up, I will go before you to Galilee" (v. 28). That's the promise. That's the message greater than our failure. After the resurrection, Jesus comes back. After the resurrection, Jesus returns to gather the scattered sheep. After the resurrection, Jesus goes before us to Galilee. Jesus goes before us into the real world, where all of us sooner or later return. He goes before us into the workplace, into the home, into every place and relationship where we find ourselves. Jesus goes before us into every place we need to be.

The story does not end in desertion. The story ends in restitution. The disciples may have deserted Jesus, but Jesus would not desert them. We may desert Jesus, but Jesus will not desert us. Since the resurrection, Jesus goes before us, and his presence is enough for us.

We don't need a "pointer." We don't need someone to stand up and point out our sins. We may deserve that kind of condemnation, but Jesus does something far better. He loves us and forgives us and redeems us. From his place on the cross, Jesus points us to God.

QUESTIONS FOR DISCUSSION/REFLECTION

1. Why did Jesus share his prediction that Peter would deny him?
2. What did Peter's response to this prediction say about Peter?
3. Why did the other disciples react as they did?
4. Have you ever felt that you denied Jesus?
5. What was the meaning of Jesus going before the disciples to Galilee after his resurrection?

CHAPTER 8

JESUS IN GETHSEMANE
Matthew 26:36-46; Mark 14:32-42; Luke 22:40-46

He said, "Abba, Father, for you all things are possible; remove this cup from me; yet, not what I want, but what you want." (Mark 14:36, NRSV)

According to Mark, Jesus prayed, "Abba, Father." In all three Gospels, Jesus asks his Father to remove the cup of suffering from him, but in Mark Jesus calls God "Abba" as well as "Father." "Abba" is the word for father in Aramaic. Paul uses the term in Romans 8:15 and Galatians 4:6. Matthew and Mark say that Jesus took Peter, James, and John with him to pray in Gethsemane. In all three Gospels, the disciples fall asleep while Jesus prays. Beyond praying for deliverance, Jesus prayed that God's will would be done. Jesus did not want to suffer, but he was willing to be betrayed into the hands of sinners if that was God's plan. Luke describes Jesus's anguish, saying his sweat "became like great drops of blood falling down on the ground" (22:44). Luke also says "an angel from heaven appeared to him and gave him strength" (22:43).

ABBA FATHER
Mark 14:36; Romans 8:15; Galatians 4:6

In counseling, Adlerian therapy features an interpretive technique called "early recollections."[1] The technique is based on the idea that what we remember from our earliest years of childhood provides clues to what is important in our lives today. A therapist who practices the psychology of Alfred Adler will ask a client to relate three or four of his or her earliest memories. Then the therapist will look for common themes, patterns, or threads in order to better understand how that client views life now.

When I studied Adlerian psychology at Bowie State University, I did the early recollections exercise, and it helped me understand myself better. One of my earliest recollections comes from the age of two. Most people can remember episodes from age three, four, or five, but my earliest memory comes from when I was two years old. I remember riding in the back seat of Jack Lowe's car, sitting on my father's lap. That's all I remember about it, but I recall that image vividly. Much later, I learned that the recollection is from a ride to the hospital. My mother was out running errands on a Saturday, leaving me in the care of my father and big sister. I was sitting in my highchair eating, and then, for just a moment, no one was watching me. I stood up in my highchair and took a swan dive onto the floor, breaking my collarbone. I don't remember that part of the story, or even being treated at the hospital, but I am told that's what happened.

What I remember is riding on my father's lap in the back seat of our neighbor's big black Buick. Obviously, I recovered, suffering no lasting ill effects from the injury. But the story achieved folklore status in our family. What fascinates me is that I remember anything about it at all. Adler said we remember what is important to us. Somehow, that memory of sitting on my father's lap must be important to me.

My father died in 2005 at the age of eighty-five after an illness of about six weeks. I was blessed to be with him (and my mother) on many occasions throughout my adult life after I was married and had children of my own. My wife and I visited him several times during the final weeks of his life, and I gave the eulogy for his funeral after his passing. Somehow, my memory of sitting on my father's lap was a clue about my relationship with my father.

Apparently, Jesus lost his father, Joseph, at some point during the early years of his life. The last mention of Joseph in the Bible is when he and Mary took twelve-year-old Jesus to the temple in Jerusalem (Luke 2:41-52). After that, Joseph is not mentioned. During Jesus's ministry, only his mother Mary is ever mentioned. Some scholars speculate that Joseph died when Jesus was a teenager. That might explain why Jesus did not begin his public ministry until the age of thirty. Perhaps he had to stay home and work to support his mother and his younger brothers and sisters until they grew up. It is probable, then, that Jesus knew what it was like to be without an earthly father. But Jesus had a Father in heaven.

There are several names for God in the New Testament. There is the Greek word for "god," *theos*, from which we get our word "theology." God is referred to as *theos* 48 times in Mark, 51 times in Matthew, 122 times in Luke, and 73 times in John. Another name for God in the New Testament is "Lord," the Greek word *kyrios*. This name for God is used 9 times in Mark, 18 times in Matthew, 37 times in Luke, and 5 times in John. Typically, God is called "Lord" in the Old Testament because the special name for God, represented by the Hebrew consonants YHWH, was too holy to pronounce aloud. Instead, the Jews called God "Lord." In many translations, YHWH is indicated in the Old Testament with capital letters: "LORD" or "Lord."

Jesus introduced another name for God: "Father." The Greek word for father is *pater*, from which we get the word "paternity." Jesus calls God "Father" 4 times in Mark, 44 times in Matthew, 15 times in Luke, and 109 times in John. As far as we know, Jesus did not speak Greek. He spoke Aramaic. So it is almost certain that Jesus used the Aramaic word for father, *abba*, to refer to God. Every time *pater* appears in the Greek text, it is probably a translation of the Aramaic word *abba*. However, one time in Mark's Gospel and two times in the letters of Paul, the original Aramaic *abba* is preserved in the Greek text. Those three passages have a deliberate redundancy, *abba pater*, "Abba Father." Even so, Jesus typically addressed God as *Abba*, as Father.

The four Gospels contain sixteen different recorded prayers of Jesus (twenty-one prayers when you count the parallels that appear in more than one Gospel). In every prayer Jesus prayed except one, he addressed God as Father. The one exception is the prayer of forsakenness that Jesus prayed from the cross: "My God, my God, why have you forsaken me?" But that prayer is actually a quotation from the 22nd Psalm. In every other prayer, Jesus addressed God as "Father," "my Father," or "our Father." The most famous prayer of Jesus, the Lord's Prayer, begins, "Our Father in heaven...." In addition to all the prayers of Jesus, the four Gospels record more than 125 other instances when Jesus referred to God as "Father." According to the *Theological Dictionary of the New Testament*, in all probability, Jesus used the word *Abba* whenever the word *pater* is used to refer to his Father in heaven.[2]

This is significant because before Jesus, hardly anyone dared to call God "Father" in a personal way. A few places in the Old Testament describe God as the Father of the Hebrew nation, but no one would have had the audacity to address God as "my Father." Biblical scholar Joachim Jeremias said there is no evidence that *abba* was ever used as a personal address to God before Jesus.[3] To the pious Jew, it would seem disrespectful, irreverent, and almost blasphemous to address God this way. *Abba* was a term of endearment used in family relationships. Jews called their own earthly fathers *abba*. When Jesus called God *Abba*, he introduced a new way of thinking about God and relating to God.

Today we naturally think about God as our Father in heaven. But that is because of Jesus. This personal sense of God's parental nature was a Christian development that originated with the teachings and prayers of Jesus. Jesus taught us to think about God as our heavenly Father. He introduced an intimacy with God that no one had dreamed of. He changed the prevailing image of God from that of a Stern Judge or Mighty Warrior to that of a Loving Father filled with mercy and forgiveness and grace.

Anne Lamott tells a story in her book *Traveling Mercies: Some Thoughts on Faith*. She writes that an airplane pilot in Alaska was sitting on a tavern barstool telling the bartender that he had lost his faith in God. The bartender asked what had caused him to lose his faith. The pilot replied that he had suffered engine failure, and his plane went down in the wilderness. The pilot survived the crash, but his radio wouldn't work, and he was stranded miles from civilization. He said, "I lay there in the wreckage, hour after hour, nearly frozen to death, crying out to God to save me, praying for help with every ounce of my being, but he didn't raise a finger to help." "But" the bartender interrupted, "you're here! You survived! You didn't die in the tundra!" The pilot replied, "Oh, some Eskimo finally came along...."[4]

Sometimes our image of God is just as truncated. When life gets difficult, how often do we blame God for our misfortune or for failing to save us or protect us? Jesus came to show us a new image of God—not a heavenly bellhop who answers to our beck and call but not a disinterested bystander either. Rather, God is our Father in heaven, who has counted the hairs on our heads and notices when even a sparrow falls to the ground. God is *Abba*, as close and dear to us as our own fathers and mothers and most cherished family members.

I think there is a reason I have that early childhood recollection of riding in the back seat of Jack Lowe's Buick. The image represents something important about my relationship with my earthly father and my relationship with my Father in heaven. My own father could not protect me from every accident and misfortune, nor does my heavenly Father protect me from all hard times. But riding on my father's lap on the way to the hospital, I knew I was going to be okay. It would take some mending, but eventually I would recover.

There is brokenness in life. A broken bone, a broken promise, a broken dream, a broken heart. But there is mending in life, too. We have a God who cares about our brokenness. We call God Abba Father, and we will never fall beneath God's everlasting arms, no matter how far we fall.

QUESTIONS FOR DISCUSSION/REFLECTION

1. Why did Jesus want the disciples to be with him in Gethsemane?
2. What did Jesus want God to do?
3. Why did the disciples fall asleep?
4. What does the word "Abba" mean to you?
5. Can you think of times in your life when God has been there for you?

NOTES

[1]For more, see "Adlerian Therapy," *Psychology Today*, updated April 27, 2022, https://www.psychologytoday.com/us/therapy-types/adlerian-therapy.

[2]Gerhard Kittel, Gerhard Friedrich, and Geoffrey William Bromiley, *Theological Dictionary of the New Testament* (10 vols.; Grand Rapids, MI: Eerdmans, 1964).

[3]See *The New Interpreter's Dictionary of the Bible*, vol. 1, p. 5.

[4]Anne Lamott, *Traveling Mercies: Some Thoughts on Faith* (New York: Pantheon Books, 1999), p. 117.

CHAPTER 9

JESUS TAKEN CAPTIVE
Matthew 26:47-56; Mark 14:43-52; Luke 22:47-53

While he was still speaking, Judas, one of the twelve, arrived; with him was a large crowd with swords and clubs, from the chief priests and the elders of the people. Now the betrayer had given them a sign, saying, "The one I will kiss is the man; arrest him." (Matthew 26:47-48, NRSV)

After leading the crowd with swords and clubs, Judas betrayed Jesus with a kiss so they would know which man to arrest. One of the disciples (John 18:10 says it was Simon Peter) drew his sword and struck the slave of the high priest, cutting off his right ear. According to Matthew, Jesus told him to put his sword back in its place, "for all who take the sword will perish by the sword" (Matt 26:52). Jesus could have appealed to his Father to send twelve legions of angels to rescue him from this arrest, but he chose to surrender peacefully in order to fulfill the scriptures of the prophets. Jesus knew it was God's purpose that he did not resist the crowd, so he remained calm. Then he watched as all the disciples deserted him and ran away. According to Mark, in addition to the disciples, a young man wearing only a linen cloth was also seized, but he shed the linen cloth and ran off naked. The young man may have been Mark himself.

BETRAYED WITH A KISS
Matthew 26:47-56

On November 26, 2005, four Christian peacemakers were taken hostage in Iraq. The group comprised one American, a Quaker from Virginia named Tom Fox; one Briton, a retired medical physicist named Norman Kember; and two Canadians, James Loney and Harmeet Singh Sooden. The four men were in Iraq under the auspices of a group called Christian Peacemaker Teams. In Baghdad, on their way to visit the Muslim Clerics Association, their vehicle was stopped about a hundred meters from the mosque where they planned to meet the Sunni religious leaders. Security officials had repeatedly warned the activists that they were taking a serious risk moving around Baghdad without armed bodyguards. Their driver and translator were left alone, but the four peacemakers were abducted.

In subsequent videos released on the Arab satellite network Al Jazeera, the four captives were accused of being spies rather than Christian peace activists and were threatened with death. Eventually that threat was carried out against one of them, as the body of American Tom Fox was discovered in a garbage dump in the western part of the city. He had been shot in the head and chest, and his throat had been slit. There also were signs of torture on his body. A couple of weeks after the discovery, the remaining three hostages were freed by multinational forces.[1]

Shortly after the kidnapping, the late conservative pundit Rush Limbaugh said on his radio show, "Part of me likes this." He explained, "Here's why I like it. I like any time a bunch of leftist feel-good handwringers are shown reality."[2]

Obviously, Rush Limbaugh looked with disdain on the mission of those four peacemakers. He branded them "leftist feel-good handwringers" who were out of touch with reality. Not everyone was so contemptuous, but others expressed reservations about the wisdom of peacemakers going into a war zone. Terry Waite, the Anglican Church hostage negotiator who himself was taken hostage in Beirut and held for five years, questioned the strategy of going into a "highly polarized" situation in Iraq. An editorial in the *Greensboro News & Record* newspaper stated, "The discovery of peace activist Tom Fox's body in Iraq…was sadly, not unexpected. But the murder…still was shocking in its senselessness and brutality." The editorial went on to say, "Fox's ideals…may seem hopelessly out of reach and completely out of touch with the realities of war."[3]

Many people wondered what those Christian peacemakers were doing in Iraq. What did they hope to accomplish? What were their objectives in being in such a dangerous place at such a dangerous time? Fox himself, the day before he was abducted, wrote a blog titled "Why We Are Here" and tried to explain the men's rationale for putting themselves in harm's way. In the last line of his electronic diary, he wrote, "We are here to stop people, including ourselves, from dehumanizing any of God's children, no matter how much they dehumanize their own souls."[4]

According to their website, Christian Peacemaker Teams was in Iraq since October 2002, "providing first-hand, independent reports from the region." They were there to train others in "non-violent intervention and human rights documentation."[5] For example, they reported the abuse of Iraqi detainees before photos from Abu Ghraib prison were ever leaked to the press. They were also involved in escorting the delivery of medicine and supplies to clinics and hospitals, ministering to families of detainees, and helping to form Islamic Peacemaker Teams. Needless to say, not everyone supported their efforts. Peacemaking in a war zone is not a popular business.

From the Christian Peacemaker Teams website, I learned that it was a Christian organization sponsored by peace-oriented denominations such as the Mennonite Church, the Church of the Brethren, and the Quakers, or Society of Friends. Now, the group is known as "Community Peacemaker Teams" to express their diversity.[6] Other church groups lent their support in Iraq, such as the Presbyterian Peace Fellowship and the Baptist Peace Fellowship of North America. Also on the website, I noticed several Bible verses quoted to lend a biblical basis for their mission. Among them I read Jesus's command to "love your enemies and pray for those who persecute you" (Matt 5:44). I also saw Paul's command to the Christians in Rome: "Do not be overcome by evil, but overcome evil with good" (Rom 12:21). And the website quoted Jesus when he said to Peter, "Put your sword back into its place; for all who take the sword will perish by the sword" (Matt 26:52). Clearly, the organization believes that the Bible justifies what they do.

Not everyone would agree. I wonder what people thought about what Jesus did that night in the Garden of Gethsemane, placing himself in such a dangerous place at such a dangerous time. Jesus knew that Judas had gone to betray him, yet Jesus remained in the garden to wait and pray. Unlike the four peace activists, Jesus did have at least one armed bodyguard who sprang to his defense when they came to seize him. Matthew doesn't identify this armed disciple, but in John's Gospel we learn that Peter drew his sword and took a swipe at the slave of the high priest, cutting off the man's ear. John even tells us the slave's name—Malchus—perhaps a detail to dissuade us from dehumanizing the enemies of Jesus.

I find it interesting that Peter carried a sword. Apparently, Jesus did not prohibit his disciples from carrying weapons. Maybe at least some of them regularly carried swords, most likely for self-defense from would-be robbers who might threaten them as they traveled. Judas knew that some of the disciples might be armed. That's why the mob he led was heavily armed, carrying swords and clubs, prepared for a fight. Had Jesus not stepped between Peter and those who had come to arrest him, there might have been a bloodbath in the Garden of Gethsemane. Peter's aim was to cut off more than an ear, no doubt, and the mob was ready to seize Jesus violently and kill anyone who got in the way. Even at the moment of his arrest, Jesus was a peacemaker, calling an end to the violence and sacrificing himself that others might be saved.

Jesus said that if he had wanted to save his own life, he could have appealed to his Father in heaven to send twelve legions of angels to rescue him. A Roman legion contained 6,000 fighting men. Jesus could have chosen to summon an angelic host of 72,000 to fight for him, but he wasn't interested in self-defense or even self-preservation. Jesus only wanted to do his Father's will. If that meant sacrificing his life so that others might be saved, he was willing to do it. So Jesus gave himself up to the mob, and the disciples deserted him and fled.

Jesus had told Peter, "Put away your sword. Those who use the sword will be killed by the sword" (Matt 26:52, NLT). Jesus would not fight, and he would not allow his disciples to fight for him. He chose to absorb evil rather than fight back. Refusing to fight back seems unnatural to us. As far as we know, Jesus never killed anybody. Perhaps the closest he came to physical violence was driving the corrupt moneychangers out of the temple with a whip of cords. Jesus did speak harshly to the hypocritical Pharisees, calling them whitewashed tombs and broods of vipers, and we may read that as a kind of verbal violence, but his anger was always righteous, never selfish. It's hard to know what Jesus would have said about the war in Iraq, but I know the violence and bloodshed would have broken his heart.

It is easy to dismiss the death of Tom Fox as a tragic consequence of a naïve Quaker being out of touch with reality. Who in his right mind would go to Iraq and try to be a peacemaker in the midst of war? But then I read about the British hostage kidnapped alongside Tom Fox, a retired medical physicist named Norman Kember. Norman is not a Quaker but a Baptist, an active member of Harrow Baptist Church in London. I went to his church's website and discovered that Norman Kember was their webmaster. His family described him as "a husband, father, and grandfather; a pacifist, promoter of human rights, a carer of other people." As a young man back in the 1950s, Norman fulfilled his national service obligations by working as a hospital porter rather than taking up arms in the military. His hospital work led to a career in medical research. He earned two doctorates and became an expert on the effects of radiation on bone growth. Before he retired, he was a professor who lectured medical students. For ten years before he went to Iraq, every Sunday after church Norman and his wife Pat went into central London to provide free food to "rough sleepers," the British term for the homeless. He also volunteered his time with the local multiple sclerosis society. Every Christmas, he encouraged his family to feed the hungry or to help in homes for the aged.

Maybe it was naïve for Norman Kember and Tom Fox and the two Canadians to go to Iraq and try to make peace. Maybe they were idealistic, unrealistic, impractical, and ill-informed. Or maybe they knew exactly what they were doing. Maybe they looked at what Jesus did—giving himself for others, rejecting violence, forgiving his enemies, doing good, sacrificing his life that others might be saved—and followed his example. In the end, Jesus would conquer not with a sword but with a cross. Jesus would win the victory over sin and death not by taking life but by giving life, his own.

A kiss is a sign of love. How fitting that Jesus was betrayed with a kiss, because love is always vulnerable and dangerous. Those who love risk being hurt by the people they love. Love is a risky business, but it is the only way to true and lasting peace. Jesus said, "Blessed are the peacemakers, for they will be called children of God" (Matt 5:9). Lord, make me an instrument of your peace.

QUESTIONS FOR DISCUSSION/REFLECTION

1. Why do you think Judas betrayed Jesus with a kiss?
2. Can you explain what Peter did?
3. Why do you think the disciples ran away?
4. What are some ways that you can be a peacemaker?
5. How was Jesus a peacemaker for us?

NOTES

[1] Robert Marus, "American Hostage Found Dead in Iraq," *Baptist Standard*, March 14, 2006, https://www.baptiststandard.com/archives/2006-archives/american-hostage-found-dead-in-iraq/.

[2] "Limbaugh Happy about Kidnapped Christians," *Toward Freedom*, December 7, 2005, https://towardfreedom.org/story/global-notebook-global-notebook/limbaugh-happy-about-kidnapped-christians/.

[3] "Fox's Fight for Peace Shouldn't Be in Vain," *Greensboro News & Record*, March 13, 2006, https://greensboro.com/editorial/editorials/fox-s-fight-for-peace-shouldn-t-be-in-vain/article_1a484fcc-3efa-5676-9999-35fdc4fd033f.html.

[4] Ibid.

[5] The group is now Community Peacemaker Teams. See https://cpt.org/about.

[6] See their website regarding the name change: https://cpt.org/about/cpt-name-change.

CHAPTER 10

JESUS BEFORE THE COUNCIL; PETER'S DENIAL
Matthew 26:57-75; Mark 14:53-72; Luke 22:54-71

After a little while the bystanders came up and said to Peter, "Certainly you are one of them, for your accent betrays you." Then he began to curse and swore an oath, "I do not know the man!" At that moment the cock crowed. Then Peter remembered what Jesus had said: "Before the cock crows, you will deny me three times." And he went out and wept bitterly. (Matthew 26:73-75, NRSV)

Judas betrayed Jesus with a kiss, and Peter denied three times that he even knew Jesus. All the disciples deserted Jesus, but the betrayal and denial were a different level of desertion. While Jesus was questioned (and accused) by the chief priests and the whole council, Peter sat outside in the courtyard. A servant girl approached him and said he was with Jesus. Peter denied it. Another servant girl said to the bystanders that Peter was with Jesus of Nazareth. Again, Peter denied it. Then the bystanders said Peter was one of the disciples. A third time, Peter denied it. When the cock crowed, Peter remembered Jesus's prediction that Peter would deny him three times. Peter left the courtyard and wept bitterly. Meanwhile, Jesus was interrogated, condemned, spat on, blindfolded, struck, and beaten. The charge against him was his claim to be the Messiah, the Son of God.

THE ROCK CRUMBLES
Matthew 26:56b-58, 69-75

All of us have regrets. We have all said something or done something that we later regret. Some of our regrets are painful, but they eventually pass. Psychologists call these "hot" regrets. They upset us for a while, but we get over them. A "hot" regret is what you feel after putting a dent in the car. It's what you feel after you break a plate washing dishes. It's what you feel after you forget a business meeting. It bothers you. You get mad at yourself for a while, but you get over it. If all we had to worry about were "hot" regrets, life would be bearable.

But another kind of regret does not pass so quickly. Psychologists call these "wistful" regrets. A "wistful" regret is hard to resolve. It stays with you a long time, maybe all your life. It's that nagging feeling in the pit of your stomach that your life would be better if only you had done something differently in the past.

Peter had a "wistful" regret after that night in the courtyard of the high priest. He followed Jesus there from the Garden of Gethsemane. All the other disciples ran away and hid after Jesus was arrested, but Peter followed at a distance. It seems like a foolish choice. He had just tried to resist Jesus's arrest. He had drawn a sword and taken a wild swipe at the high priest's servant, cutting off his right ear in the process. Why would Peter go to the high priest's house after that? Of all the disciples, Peter should have hidden. But he followed Jesus in the night.

We should not be too hasty to label Peter a coward, for what he did took a lot of courage. Somebody might have recognized him. In fact, somebody did. He stood there in the courtyard in the wee hours of the morning, and a servant girl approached him. "You were with Jesus," she said accusingly. Peter replied, "I don't know what you're talking about." Then, unsure he had convinced her with his denial, he backed out of the courtyard to the front porch. Another servant girl spotted him and said to the bystanders, "This guy was with Jesus of Nazareth." Peter again vehemently denied it. "I don't even know the man," Peter said. A little while later, some people walked over to Peter and said, "We know you're one of them. We can tell because you have a Galilean accent." Curses began to spew from Peter's mouth, and he swore, "I don't know that man!"

Before another word was said, a rooster crowed. Peter remembered Jesus's prediction only hours earlier: "Before a rooster crows, you will deny me three times." How could he have done such a thing? With wistful regret, Peter went out and wept bitterly.

This story amazes not because Peter failed Jesus but because *the Bible tells us* that Peter failed Jesus. Even more amazing is the possibility that this account came from Peter himself. Only Peter knew the full story of what he did and said. Peter must have told this story about himself, and that is how it was included in the four Gospels. Certainly, Peter was not proud of what he did. It seems he would try to cover it up or forget about it. But Peter thought it was important for others to know about his failures, so Matthew, Mark, Luke, and John give us their versions of this sad event. Why would Peter let us witness his regrettable moment of denial? Because at times in our lives, we fail Jesus too.

We've all been there. We've all said and done things we later regretted. In our Christian walk, in our family life, in our relationships at work or school, and in our friendships, we have all failed Jesus at one time or another. Sometimes we even denied that we know Jesus.

A man felt guilty for keeping silent about his faith. He knew God wanted him to tell others about Jesus, but he it was hard for him to work up the courage to speak a verbal witness. Every morning he said the same prayer: "Lord, if you want me to witness to someone today, give me a sign to show me who it is." One day he took the bus to work. The bus had plenty of empty seats, but a big, burly fellow came and sat next to him. Before the timid Christian could say anything, the big guy burst into tears. He turned and said, "My life is falling apart. I'm a lost sinner and I need the Lord. Can you tell me how to be saved?" The reluctant witness bowed his head and asked, "Lord, is this a sign?"

My guess is that most of us have failed Christ when it comes to sharing our faith with others. Most of us have plenty of opportunities to tell other people about Jesus, invite people to church, or serve others in Christ's name. But we're too busy, too shy, or too preoccupied to let other people know where we stand in terms of our relationship with Jesus Christ. Sometimes, like Peter, we even deny we know Jesus, if not by our words then by our actions.

An old hymn says, "Let others see Jesus in you."[1] But do they? Do they see Christ in the things we say and do? Peter was not the only believer to deny Christ. All of us have failed Jesus at some point in our lives, and all of us should feel the same wistful regret.

This story is included in the Gospels to provide a ray of hope. Peter failed Jesus miserably, but this was not the end of the story. We know that Peter later became a courageous leader in the church. That happened because he was truly sorry for failing Jesus, and Jesus forgave Peter for denying him. This is the ray of hope for us. If we are truly sorry for our failures, Jesus will forgive us too. We don't have to stay stuck in a rut of denial. We can be forgiven, and we can grow in our faith as a result of the times when we let Jesus down.

In truth, all the disciples failed Jesus that night—they all ran out on him. Judas was also sorry for what he did; in fact, he was so filled with regret that he tried to give back the money he was paid to betray Jesus. But while Judas was truly sorry, he did not accept the forgiveness that Christ offered. Instead, he went out and hanged himself. Peter accepted Christ's forgiveness, and that made all the difference. That can make all the difference in our lives, too—accepting the forgiveness that Christ offers us.

Psychologists have discovered that what people regret most is not the things they have done but rather the things they have failed to do. But this can be a day of no regrets. This can be a day of accepting Christ's forgiveness and growing in his grace. Remember that Jesus gave his all that we might have new life.

QUESTIONS FOR DISCUSSION/REFLECTION

1. Why do you think Peter denied Jesus?
2. When you read about what Jesus suffered, can you fathom the depth of his love for us?
3. Can you think of times when you have failed Jesus?
4. How can you accept the forgiveness Jesus offers?
5. How can failure become a way to growth?

NOTE

[1] B. B. McKinney (1886–1952), "Let Others See Jesus in You," Hymnary.org, https://hymnary.org/text/while_passing_through_this_world_of_sin.

CHAPTER 11

JESUS DELIVERED TO PILATE
Matthew 27:1-2; Mark 15:1; Luke 23:1+

As soon as it was morning, the chief priests held a consultation with the elders and scribes and the whole council. They bound Jesus, led him away, and handed him over to Pilate. (Mark 15:1, NRSV)

The deal was done. In order to bring about his death, Jesus was handed over to the Roman governor, Pontius Pilate, who ruled over Judea, Samaria, and Idumaea. The Sanhedrin had taken formal action in a pre-dawn hearing. The charge against Jesus was made to sound like treason, an offense the Roman government punished by death. The idea was to portray Jesus not as a dissenter to Jewish religious doctrines but as a political opponent to the Roman empire. The Jewish leaders wanted to get rid of Jesus, and they aimed to use Pilate and the Roman authorities to do it.

GOD AND GOVERNMENT
Mark 15:1

My friend Dr. Dan Ivins preceded me as pastor of Village Baptist Church in Bowie, Maryland, where he served for ten years. After leaving Village, Brother Dan pastored churches in Alabama, back in Maryland, then in Arizona, Oregon, and New York. His final full-time pastorate was at The First Baptist Church in America in Providence, Rhode Island, where he served from 2006–2014. This church is called "The First Baptist Church in America" because, historically, it was. Roger Williams founded the church in 1638. According to the church's website, "The story of this church begins with Roger Williams, one of the thousands of Puritans who departed from England in the 1630's to escape religious and political repression at the hands of the King and the Church of England."[1]

Roger Williams was born in London, possibly in 1603.[2] The year is not certain because his birth records were destroyed in the Great Fire of London in 1666. Williams was raised in the Church of England, but he became a Puritan when he studied at Cambridge. Like many Puritans, Williams and his wife immigrated to the New World in 1631 to escape religious persecution in England. Williams believed in religious freedom, that all persons should be free to follow their own beliefs without mandates from church or government authorities. Williams progressed from being a Puritan and seeking to purify the Church of England to becoming a Separatist and seeking to separate completely from the Church of England, believing it to be corrupt.

Williams had contact and discussions with the churches in Boston and Salem, but he and his wife settled in Plymouth Colony, and they got involved in the church there. However, Williams began to conclude that the church was not sufficiently separated from the Church of England. Plus, his contact with the indigenous Narragansett people led him to question the colonial charters that seized Native American lands. So Williams moved back to Salem, but Massachusetts Bay authorities became alarmed by his "erroneous" and "dangerous" opinions.

Eventually Williams was tried by the General Court and convicted of sedition and heresy. He was expelled from Salem and the authorities made plans to send him back to England. Williams managed to escape, and he spent the winter with some Wampanoag people who offered him shelter. In 1636, Williams and some like-minded followers founded a new settlement that they called Providence Plantations, designed to be a place of welcome for those "distressed of conscience." Purchasing land from some Native Americans, Williams built a shelter and sent for his wife and two small children to join him there. After holding religious services in his home for nearly a year, he founded what would become the first Baptist church in America in 1638. Early in 1639, after studying the New Testament and concluding that infant baptism was not in the scriptures, Williams was the first to be baptized as a believer, and others in the church followed. Their believer's baptisms made the congregation the first Baptist church in America.

By 1640, Providence included almost forty families. The community needed to form some sort of government. The people agreed to a compact based on the ideals of religious freedom and the separation of church and state. This new colony "became a haven for those seeking religious freedom."[3] Although Williams himself did not remain a Baptist for long, the Baptist church that he had founded continued, along with the ideals of religious liberty and the separation of church and state.

Such ideals were later incorporated into the founding of the United States of America. The first amendment to the US Constitution prevents the government from making laws to establish religion or to prevent the free exercise of religion. In other words, God and government are not to be mixed. These were radical ideas. Even today, the Church of England is still connected to the English government, but in America church and the state are separate. People are free to follow the religious convictions of their own consciences, not the dictates of religious establishments or government authorities.

When Jesus was delivered to Pilate, religion and politics were profoundly mixed. Religious authorities seized Jesus and delivered him to the political authorities for conviction and execution. The religious authorities had already convicted Jesus of heresy, and they delivered Jesus to Pilate under the pretense that Jesus posed a threat to the political establishment. This mixture of religion and politics would become deadly for Jesus.

Pontius Pilate was not a Jew. He was the Roman prefect of Judea who played a central role in the trial and crucifixion of Jesus. Pilate had little regard for the religion of the Jews and was known to use brutal force to suppress any dissent. The Jewish leaders (the chief priests, elders, scribes, and council) conspired to eliminate Jesus by handing him over to Pilate as a proposed threat to Rome.

What had Jesus done to threaten the Jewish leaders? Plenty. What he taught diverged from their orthodoxy and their authority. They saw Jesus as a threat to their power over the people. Just as Roger Williams was perceived as a threat to the religious and political leaders of Massachusetts Bay Colony, Jesus was perceived as a threat to the religious and political Jewish leaders in Jerusalem. But rather than deciding to send Jesus back to where he came from (Nazareth)—as the leaders of Massachusetts Bay sought to send Roger Williams back to England—the Jews wanted to get rid of Jesus once and for all by having him executed. Thus, they delivered Jesus to Pilate to have Jesus killed.

Roger Williams knew firsthand about the dangers of mixing religion and politics. He was expelled from Salem because of his religious views regarding the Church of England as well as his political views regarding the Native Americans. Thus, when Williams founded the new community at Providence, he wanted to make sure religion and government would not be mixed. Thus, he worked to ensure religious liberty and the separation of church and state.

Like Roger Williams, Jesus was a victim of religious persecution. Unlike Williams, Jesus did not escape those who wanted to get rid of him. Rather, Jesus gave himself for us all.

QUESTIONS FOR DISCUSSION/REFLECTION

1. Why do you think the Jewish leaders decided to deliver Jesus to Pilate?
2. What are the dangers of mixing religion and politics?
3. Can you think of ways that the separation of church and state is threatened today?
4. Do churches sometimes threaten religious liberty?
5. What is the ultimate religious authority for you?

NOTES

[1] "The Prophet of Religious Freedom," *The First Baptist Church in America*, https://www.firstbaptistchurchinamerica.org/history/the-prophet-of-religious-freedom/.

[2] The information about Roger Williams is drawn from Pamela R. Durso and Keith E. Durso, *The Story of Baptists in the United States* (Brentwood, TN: Baptist History and Heritage Society, 2006).

[3] Ibid., 26-29.

CHAPTER 12

THE DEATH OF JUDAS
Matthew 27:3-10

> *When Judas, his betrayer, saw that Jesus was condemned, he repented and brought back the thirty pieces of silver to the chief priests and the elders. He said, "I have sinned by betraying innocent blood." But they said, "What is that to us? See to it yourself." Throwing down the pieces of silver in the temple, he departed; and then he went and hanged himself. (Matthew 27:3-5, NRSV)*

Only Matthew tells us about the death of Judas. Mark and Luke say nothing about it in their Gospels. Luke does include an account in the Acts of the Apostles. In Acts 1:16-18, Luke tells about Judas's betrayal. He quotes Peter, who said, "Now this man acquired a field with the reward of his wickedness; and falling headlong, he burst open in the middle and all his bowels gushed out" (v. 18). Whether this account of Judas's death can be squared with Matthew's version that Judas hanged himself is open to question. The word for "hanged" can also mean "impaled." In Acts, Peter gives this description of what became of Judas. Whether he hanged himself or impaled himself (and burst open and his bowels gushed out), Judas died, and the "blood money" he was given was used to buy a field as a place to bury foreigners. That's why the burial place was called the "Field of Blood." Matthew says this was the fulfillment of prophecy. The thirty pieces of silver are mentioned in Zechariah 11:12-13. The potter's field is referenced in Jeremiah 18:2-3 and 32:6-15.

THE FIELD OF BLOOD
Matthew 27:3-10; Acts 1:15-20

I retired in 2018 after forty-one years of full-time pastoral ministry. My last tenure was at Village Baptist Church in Bowie, Maryland, where I served as pastor for thirty-three years. After I retired, I wrote a book, *Preaching for the Long Haul: A Case Study on Long-Term Pastoral Ministry*.[1] I thought that would be all I had to say; then the COVID pandemic hit. With plenty of time on my hands, I began to write a series of Bible study books titled "Spelunking Scripture." This book is the latest in that series.

Near the end of the pandemic (although it may never really end), I got an idea for another book. It's a book of eulogies I have given over the years for funerals, memorial services, and graveside committal services. During the pandemic, I gave eulogies for seven such services. Several of the funerals were held outside at cemeteries due to safety protocols. Funerals held inside required precautions such as social distancing, face masks, and limited attendance. Such changes in funeral customs accentuated the importance of eulogies to comfort grieving families.

The book of eulogies is titled *The Barefoot Eulogist: Speaking a Good Word While Standing on Holy Ground*.[2] That is how I feel every time I give a eulogy—I speak a good word (from the Greek, *eu logos*), and I am "barefoot" because I stand on holy ground. The eulogies I selected for the book represent different circumstances of the persons being remembered. I contacted family members for their permission to include the eulogies of their loved ones in the book.

The book includes two eulogies for people who died of COVID-19. It includes eulogies for people who died later in life but who lived exemplary Christian lives. It includes eulogies for people who died in the prime of life. It includes eulogies for people who died in tragic circumstances, such as a father and his ten-year-old daughter who were killed in a car accident. It includes the eulogy for a baby who died at five months of age. As I said, in each case, I received permission from surviving family members to include the eulogy of their loved one. After the book was published, many of those family members wrote to thank me for including the eulogy of their loved one as a way to remember them.

When I told my mother about the book, she asked if I included a eulogy for someone who died by suicide. "No," I said. I have given a eulogy for someone who died by suicide. I tell about it in the second chapter of my book, *Spelunking Scripture: The Letters of Paul*, on pages 9–10. I do not identify the person who died in order to protect surviving family members. That is why I did not include that person's eulogy in *The Barefoot Eulogist*. I did not feel it was appropriate to ask her loved ones for permission to include it. Suicide is simply too painful for surviving family members. When a loved one dies by suicide, there is not only grief for family members and friends, but there is often also guilt. Survivors inevitably ask themselves, "What could I have done?"

We don't know if Judas had surviving family members, but he did have friends, namely the other disciples of Jesus. We know from the Gospel accounts that they did not feel guilty about not doing something to help Judas. They felt angry that Judas had betrayed Jesus (and stolen from the common purse). Never mind that all of them failed Jesus in some way. Peter denied he even knew Jesus, and all the other disciples ran away and hid after Jesus's arrest. My guess is that despite their own failings, they thought Judas had failed Jesus the worst, and thus he deserved to die for his betrayal. They probably thought Judas had it coming.

But that's not what Jesus was about. Jesus was not about punishing people for their sins. He was about loving people and forgiving them for their sins. It's clear that Jesus was hurt that Judas chose to betray him. But no doubt Jesus was hurt that Peter denied him and that the other disciples ran out on him. The failure of all the disciples was a part of Jesus's passion, a part of his suffering. Yet Jesus suffered out of love for all of us.

The money Judas was given for betraying Jesus was used to buy a field for burying foreigners. It was called the Field of Blood. We don't know where Judas was buried or if he was even buried at all. All four Gospels and the book of Acts portray Judas as the "bad guy" of the story. But his regret over what he did presents a more complicated picture of Judas. Apparently, he repented of his betrayal of Jesus. Yet Judas could not forgive himself, so he took his own life. He came to recognize who Jesus was—God's Son—but he did not understand why Jesus had come: to forgive.

Suicide is a tragedy because it means someone has given up hope. But Jesus came to give us hope, regardless of the circumstances of our lives. That does not mean everything will turn out well. As I mentioned, in the book of eulogies I wrote, I included eulogies for people who died tragic deaths. The father and his ten-year-old daughter who died in the auto accident were tragic deaths. The widow lost her husband and only child. Everyone who knew them grieved their deaths. Yet somehow those who grieved found the grace to carry on.

The baby who died at five months of age was a tragic loss for his family. Yet, somehow, his parents and grandparents and his sibling and all who care about the family found the grace to carry on. Hope does not eliminate the tragedies of life, but hope gives us the grace to carry on. In the eulogy for the baby, I said, we "are not going to get over this." Rather, we "will be forever changed by his life and his passing. The question is: what kind of change will we experience? Will this experience make us angry or bitter or despairing? Or will this experience make us kinder and more compassionate and more loving and more appreciative of life?"[3]

The suicide of Judas is about more than a bad guy getting what he deserved. It's about regret and what we do with it. Peter regretted denying Jesus. He went out and wept bitterly when he recognized his failure. But that was not the end of Peter's story. Somehow, Peter became a leader in the early church. Somehow, he was able to move past his failure. Peter was able to receive forgiveness, grow in grace, and find new meaning for his life. Failure was not the final word.

Maybe the Field of Blood is a sign of Judas's redemption. Somehow, the tragic ending of his life was used for something. Somehow, the thirty pieces of silver became more than payment for betrayal. Somehow, God used Judas's death for good.

QUESTIONS FOR DISCUSSION/REFLECTION

1. Why do you think Judas betrayed Jesus?
2. Why did Judas regret what he had done?
3. Why do you think Judas took his own life?
4. What do you think happened to Judas after he died?
5. What is the meaning of the Field of Blood?

NOTES

[1] *Preaching for the Long Haul* (Macon, GA: Nurturing Faith, 2019).
[2] *The Barefoot Eulogist* (Macon, GA: Nurturing Faith, 2022).
[3] Ibid., 32.

CHAPTER 13

THE TRIAL BEFORE PILATE
Matthew 27:11-14; Mark 15:2-5; Luke 23:2-5

> *Now Jesus stood before the governor; and the governor asked him, "Are you the King of the Jews?" Jesus said, "You say so." But when he was accused by the chief priests and elders, he did not answer. Then Pilate said to him, "Do you not hear how many accusations they make against you?" But he gave no answer, not even to a single charge, so that the governor was greatly amazed. (Matthew 27:11-14, NRSV)*

Jesus did not seek to defend himself in the trial before Pilate. According to Luke, the chief priests and elders accused Jesus of perverting the nation, forbidding people to pay taxes to the emperor, and saying that he was the Messiah, a king. Pilate asked Jesus directly if he was the King of the Jews. Jesus responded cryptically, "You say so." Pilate was amazed that Jesus would not answer the charges against him. What kind of a trial is possible when the defendant remains silent? Of course, Jesus knew the trial was rigged. He could give no answer to satisfy the Jewish authorities, and Pilate was basically an outsider who would do anything necessary to maintain order and remain in power.

TRUTH ON TRIAL
Matthew 27:11-31

In 2006, two trials made international headlines. One was held in Alexandria, Virginia. The defendant was Zacarias Moussaoui, an admitted conspirator in the Al-Qaeda attacks on America. In riveting testimony, Moussaoui claimed that he and would-be shoe bomber Richard Reid were supposed to have hijacked a fifth airplane on September 11, 2001, and flown it into the White House. Richard Reid tried to detonate a bomb in his shoe aboard a transatlantic flight from Paris to Miami. Fellow passengers stopped him, and the plane was diverted to Boston, where Reid was arrested.

Moussaoui could not take part in the 9/11 attacks in 2001 because he had been arrested a month earlier on immigration violations. Before Moussaoui took the stand, his court-appointed defense lawyers tried to stop him from testifying. They argued that since Moussaoui only recognized Islamic law, and since he had contempt for the American judicial system, he would not be a competent witness. There was no question about Moussaoui's guilt. The only question was whether he would get the death penalty or life in prison. Zacarias Moussaoui is currently serving a life sentence without possibility of parole.[1]

Another high-profile trial took place half a world away in Afghanistan. The person on trial there was not an Al-Qaeda operative but an Afghan who had converted from Islam to Christianity. His name was Abdul Rahman, but he too faced the death penalty if convicted. Had his case not provoked a storm of protests from Western governments, Rahman probably would have been executed. Under Islamic law, it is a crime to reject Islam or to convert to another religion. Islamic law says that converting from Islam is blasphemy and apostasy, punishable by death.[2]

Abdul Rahman became a Christian while working with a Christian relief agency that was helping Afghan refugees in Pakistan. Unable to go home, he lived in Germany for years when the Taliban were driven out of power by the US invasion of Afghanistan. After returning to his home country in 2002, he kept his religious beliefs to himself. It was like an Afghan version of "Don't Ask, Don't Tell."

Rahman's religion became a legal issue when a family dispute over custody of his children came to the attention of the authorities. Rahman was discovered to be in possession of a Bible. He was arrested and held in a maximum-security prison on the outskirts of Kabul. His family figured he must be insane to have converted from Islam to Christianity. But Rahman refused to recant and boldly proclaimed, "I believe in Christ, and I am a Christian." Ironically, the charge that he was insane, along with intense pressure from the US government and other nations to resolve the situation peacefully, saved him from execution.

The matter was resolved when Rahman was granted political asylum in Italy and spirited out of Afghanistan, despite the demands of prominent Muslim clerics that he be forced to convert back to Islam or be executed. So the world watched the trial in Afghanistan and the trial in Virginia to see if justice was done.

Like Zacarias Moussaoui and Abdul Rahman, Jesus was on trial for his life. Like them, Jesus refused to deny the charges against him. Perhaps it would have been pointless for Jesus to deny the charges, for nothing he said would have changed the intent of the chief priests and the elders to have him killed. Their main accusation against him was blasphemy, but the Romans would care little about a religious dispute. So the Jewish leaders came up with a charge that the Romans could not ignore, namely, treason against the state. They accused Jesus of seeking to usurp the power of Rome by aspiring to be the King of the Jews.

The Trial Before Pilate

Never mind that Jesus had no political ambitions. The Roman governor, Pontius Pilate, was obligated to protect Roman authority and keep order at any cost. If that meant sending an innocent man to death, so be it.

Pilate was the Roman prefect of Judea from AD 26–36. The Roman government must have been satisfied with his performance since he governed Judea for an unusually long tenure. He was known to use brutal force to repress any dissent. He was not a friend of the Jewish people. When he first brought Roman troops into Jerusalem, they carried busts of the emperor. This was an offense to the Jews because the busts were considered idolatrous images. Pilate also used temple funds to build an aqueduct. It's no wonder that Pilate and Herod were enemies before they met Jesus (Luke 23:12).

Pilate was amazed that Jesus refused to defend himself, especially since the charges against him seemed without merit. Even Pilate's wife had misgivings about condemning Jesus. She had a foreboding dream about the accused, and she warned Pilate to "have nothing to do with that innocent man" (Matt 27:19). The Romans viewed dreams as a way for the gods to communicate an important message. But Pilate had more pressing concerns than heeding a message from his wife. He could ill afford to show mercy to one accused of being an enemy of the state. He shared his wife's belief that Jesus was innocent, but the Jewish leaders had him in a bind. If he judged Jesus to be innocent and let him go, the Jewish leaders could accuse Pilate of being soft on treason.

Truth was on trial. Truth is always on trial. Did Zacarias Moussaoui conspire against the United States government? He proudly admitted that he did. Did Abdul Rahman convert from Islam to Christianity? Yes, he said, "I believe in Christ, and I am a Christian." Was Jesus the "King of the Jews"? Jesus replied to Pilate, "You say so."

Pilate was amazed that Jesus did not answer the charges against him. Pilate would consider Jesus to be innocent, but he would convict Jesus anyway because he didn't really care about the truth. Pilate only cared about protecting himself, preserving his own authority, and remaining in power.

QUESTIONS FOR DISCUSSION/REFLECTION

1. Was Jesus the "King of the Jews"?
2. Why did Pilate question Jesus?
3. Why do you think Jesus did not answer the charges against him?
4. Why did the chief priests and elders see Jesus as a threat?
5. What did Pilate really think about Jesus?

NOTES

[1] Matthew Barakat, "Moussaoui testifies he was to fly 5th plane into White House," *Associated Press*, March 27, 2006.

[2] "Defending Abdul Rahman," *Chicago Tribune*, March 25, 2006, https://www.chicagotribune.com/2006/03/25/defending-abdul-rahman/.

CHAPTER 14

JESUS BEFORE HEROD
Luke 23:6-16

When Herod saw Jesus, he was very glad, for he had been wanting to see him for a long time, because he had heard about him, and was hoping to see him perform some sign. He questioned him at some length, but Jesus gave him no answer. The chief priests and the scribes stood by, vehemently accusing him. Even Herod and his soldiers treated him with contempt and mocked him; then he put an elegant robe on him, and sent him back to Pilate. (Luke 23:8-11, NRSV)

According to Luke, Pilate sent Jesus to Herod, since as a Galilean Jesus was under Herod's jurisdiction. Herod was in Jerusalem at the time, and Pilate probably thought he could pass the buck by sending Jesus his way. Herod was glad to interrogate Jesus since he had heard for a long time about this wonder-working preacher from Nazareth. Herod hoped Jesus would perform some sign, kind of like a magic show. Herod questioned Jesus, but Jesus would not cooperate. All the while, the chief priests and scribes stood by, hurling accusations at Jesus. Herod and his soldiers joined in mocking Jesus and treating him with contempt. As an act of ironic indignity, they put an elegant robe on Jesus, befitting his claim to be "King of the Jews." Then Herod sent Jesus back to Pilate.

As a result, Herod and Pilate became friends rather than enemies. In Jesus, they shared a common foe, a troublemaker they needed to get rid of. Still, Pilate had a problem. He had not found Jesus guilty of any charges leveled by the chief priests and other leaders. Since Herod sent Jesus back to Pilate, apparently Herod had not found Jesus guilty either. So, since neither Pilate nor Herod deemed Jesus of deserving death, Pilate resolved to have Jesus flogged (for the trouble) and then release him. This was to fulfill Pilate's obligation to release a prisoner at the Passover festival.

WHO IS THE KING OF THE JEWS?
Luke 23:6-16

Herod was not a good guy. After his father Herod the Great died in 4 BC, the Roman emperor Augustus Caesar divided Herod's kingdom among three of his sons—Herod Archelaus, Herod Antipas, and Herod Philip. Herod Antipas was made ruler of Galilee and Perea. He ruled from 4 BC until AD 39. During that time, he exercised his authority ruthlessly. When John the Baptist began to challenge that authority, Herod Antipas had John arrested, bound in chains, and thrown into prison. John had criticized Herod for taking his brother Philip's wife, Herodias. Herod would have killed John then, but he feared the crowds who regarded John as a prophet.

But when Herod's birthday came, the daughter of Herodias danced at the party. Herod was so pleased with her performance that he promised to give her whatever she wanted. Her mother prompted her to ask for the head of John the Baptist on a platter. Herod wasn't expecting that, but he sent a soldier to behead John in prison. Then he presented John's head on a platter to the girl, and she gave it to her mother (Matt 14:3-12; Mark 6:17-29).

When Herod heard about Jesus and all the wonders he was doing, he thought John the Baptist had come back from the dead. Such was the beginning of Herod's fascination with (and fear of) Jesus.

Herod Antipas was a chip off the block of his father, Herod the Great. The elder Herod had so curried the favor of Rome that in 40 BC the Roman Senate appointed him king of the Jews. The name "Herod" was Greek, not Hebrew. Though technically Jewish, Herod's family was from Idumea, and his ancestors had been forced to convert to Judaism by Jon Hyrcanus (son of Simon Maccabeus) in the second century BC. Herod the Great's complete loyalty to Rome enabled him to rule over the Jews from 40–4 BC. He gained some support among the Jews with his building projects, especially after he began to rebuild the temple in 20 BC.

After Jesus's birth, magi came to Jerusalem inquiring about the child born king of the Jews. Herod the Great was frightened about a potential rival to his throne. Upon learning that the child was born in Bethlehem, Herod was determined to search for the child to destroy him. Herod's method was to order the deaths of all children in and around Bethlehem who were two years old or under. Jesus escaped the massacre of the innocents because his father Joseph was warned in a dream to flee.

Herod the Great's murder of the children in Bethlehem was not out of character. He had one of his ten wives, Mariamne, killed, along with two of their sons—Alexander and Aristobulus—as well as Antipater, a son by another wife,

Jesus Before Herod

Doris. A king who would kill members of his own family would not hesitate to eliminate any other potential rivals to his throne.

Upon Herod the Great's death in 4 BC, three of his sons were appointed to succeed him, though none of them was pronounced king of the Jews. Herod Archelaus was named Ethnarch of Judea, Sumaria, and Idumea. Herod Antipas was named Tetrarch of Galilee and Perea. Herod Philip was named Tetrarch of Batanea, Trachonitis, and Auranitis. As sons of Herod the Great, none of them were men of virtue, but they were men consumed with the quest for power and control.

Why did Pilate send Jesus to Herod Antipas? Because Herod was Tetrarch of Galilee, and Jesus was a Galilean. The rock opera *Jesus Christ Superstar* is loosely based on the accounts of the Passion in the Gospels. In the 1973 musical, a song titled "Pilate and Christ" depicts Pilate's interrogation of Jesus before he sent him to Herod. The lyrics, by Andrew Lloyd Webber, seem to be based on that encounter.

> Since you come from Galilee, then you need not come to me
> You're Herod's race! You're Herod's case!

So Pilate sent Jesus to Herod. Herod conducted his own interrogation of Jesus with similar results. Jesus gave Herod no answer; after treating Jesus with contempt and mocking him, Herod sent him back to Pilate. No doubt, Herod wanted to be king of the Jews himself. He probably figured he could get rid of Jesus by sending him back to Pilate. Neither Herod nor Pilate had found Jesus guilty of the charges against him, leveled by the chief priests and scribes. That's why Pilate declared he would have Jesus flogged and released. But that was not the end of the story.

QUESTIONS FOR DISCUSSION/REFLECTION

1. Do you think Herod was threatened by Jesus?
2. Why did Herod want to see Jesus?
3. Why do you think Jesus did not answer the charges against him?
4. Why did Herod send Jesus back to Pilate?
5. Who was the King of the Jews?

CHAPTER 15

THE SENTENCE OF DEATH
Matthew 27:15-26; Mark 15:6-15; Luke 23:17-25

> *Now a man called Barabbas was in prison with the rebels who had committed murder during the insurrection. So the crowd came and began to ask Pilate to do for them according to his custom. Then he answered them, "Do you want me to release for you the King of the Jews?" But the chief priests stirred up the crowd to have him release Barabbas for them instead. "Then what do you wish me to do with the man you call the King of the Jews?" They shouted back, "Crucify him!" (Mark 15:7-9, 11-13, NRSV)*

Pilate had a custom of releasing a prisoner to the Jewish people during the festival of the Passover, anyone they wanted. Pilate saw it as an opportunity to release Jesus, since neither Pilate nor Herod had found him guilty of the charges leveled against him by the chief priests and the elders. Pilate said, "He has done nothing to deserve death" (Luke 23:15b). He intended to have Jesus flogged and then released. But the chief priests and elders persuaded the crowds to ask for Pilate to release a notorious prisoner named Jesus Barabbas. Barabbas was in prison for insurrection and murder. Pilate was dumbfounded. Why would they choose Barabbas over Jesus? And why would they want Jesus to be crucified? Pilate asked, "Why, what evil has he done?" But they shouted even louder, "Crucify him!" So, to satisfy the crowd, Pilate released Barabbas, had Jesus flogged, then handed Jesus over to be crucified.

THE PEOPLE'S CHOICE
Mark 15:1-15

I'm old enough to remember the Soviet Union. For the first forty years of my life, it was the chief threat against the United States. As a nuclear power, the Soviet Union had to be taken seriously. In the early 1980s, there was a succession of Soviet leaders. After Leonid Brezhnev died in 1982, he was succeeded by Yuri Andropov, who died in 1984. Then Konstantin Chernenko succeeded Andropov, but he died the following year in 1985. After his passing, Mikhail Gorbachev ascended to the head of the Communist Party in the Soviet Union. Three times in just over two years, the Soviet leader died, touching off an intriguing power struggle within the Soviet Politburo. Each time, we wondered whom they would choose and how it would affect the rest of the world. In a nuclear age, that kind of choice can mean the difference between life and death for every person on the face of the earth.

As it turned out, Gorbachev played a crucial role in what happened next. Under his leadership, in 1991 the Soviet Union began to disassemble, with many former Soviet republics becoming independent nations. Yet Russia has remained a nuclear rival to the United States, and in our time the war in Ukraine has reminded us that vestiges and aspirations of the Soviet empire remain.

A long time ago in the city of Jerusalem, outside the palace of the Roman procurator Pontius Pilate, the people made a choice with even more at stake. Of course, they did not know it at the time. It seemed rather simple and not that important. The choice: to release a carpenter's son from Nazareth or a renowned Jewish freedom fighter; an obscure rabbi from Galilee or a nationalistic zealot; Jesus or Barabbas. It seemed like a simple choice, but oh the difference that choice made.

This part of the passion story contains some fascinating details that we dare not miss. Above all, we should not miss the irony of the story. We know little about this man named Barabbas except that he was imprisoned for insurrection and murder. Apparently, he was a member of a terrorist group that tried to force the Romans out of Palestine through assassinations and other acts of violence. If Barabbas were alive today, he probably would be a member of Hamas or Al-Qaeda or some other terrorist organization. This is where the irony begins. Barabbas, the convicted insurrectionist, was set free, while Jesus, accused of insurrection, died in his place.

But there's more. Jesus and Barabbas stood for entirely different things. Jesus was a man of love, while Barabbas was a man of hate. Jesus stood for peace, while Barabbas practiced violence. Jesus came to fulfill the law, while Barabbas came to break the law. Jesus represented a heavenly, spiritual kingdom, while Barabbas fought for an earthly, political kingdom. Jesus came to win people's hearts, while Barabbas sought to force people's hands. Jesus healed, while Barabbas destroyed. Jesus represented the truth, while Barabbas practiced deception. Jesus saved people from death, while Barabbas sent people to death. Jesus forgave sin, while Barabbas committed sin.

At almost every point, Jesus and Barabbas had entirely different approaches to life, and yet the people chose Barabbas. That tells us something about human nature and about us as well.

Why did the people choose Barabbas? There are several possible explanations. The crowd outside of Pilate's palace may have been supporters of Barabbas. Perhaps they were terrorist sympathizers; perhaps they had gathered to try to win his release. Or, as Mark implies, maybe the chief priests assembled the crowd. Maybe the Jewish authorities orchestrated the whole thing. Maybe the priests were moving in and out among the people, inciting their emotions and telling them what to say. Whatever the reason, when given a clear choice, the crowd chose Barabbas. In effect, they chose evil instead of goodness, hate instead of love, lies instead of truth, destruction instead of healing, violence instead of peace, death instead of life. The people chose Barabbas, and the irony continues.

The name "Barabbas" has an interesting meaning. Literally, Barabbas, *bar abba*, means "son of the father." Jesus of Nazareth, the Son of God, was "Son of the Father." Do you see the irony? The people chose to free a man named Barabbas, son of the father, but they condemned to death the true Son of the Father. And there's more.

According to some early manuscripts of Matthew's Gospel, Barabbas's full name is given as "Jesus Barabbas." It's possible that Barabbas, the son of the father, was named Jesus too. Jesus was a fairly common name back then, so it is possible that Barabbas's given name was Jesus. Some scholars have speculated that pious Christian scribes deleted "Jesus" from his name because they could not stand the thought of Barabbas having the same name as our Lord.

So the irony is greater still: two Jesuses, two sons of the father, Jesus Barabbas and Jesus of Nazareth, two would-be kingdom makers, two revolutionaries, two threats to the status quo. Yet they represented two entirely different ways of approaching life. And the people chose Barabbas.

Could it be that this choice is still made today? Could it be that we choose Jesus, or we choose Barabbas, by the decisions we make every day? Every time we give in to selfish desires, that is a Barabbas choice. Every time we try to take shortcuts or take the easy way out, we choose Barabbas. Every time we lie or cheat or deceive, we choose Barabbas. Every time we look down on other people or scheme to get our own way, we choose Barabbas.

In fact, there is probably a mixture of Barabbas and Jesus in all of us. There is within each of us a combination of evil impulses and good intentions, of hateful ideas and loving motives. We are neither all Barabbas nor all Jesus but some of each. No matter how hard we try, there is a Barabbas dimension to each of us. We try to be good people, but we mess up. We speak a word in anger, or we give in to selfish pride. We take our friends and family for granted, or we turn our backs on the needs of others. We hoard our money or spend it foolishly on things that don't really matter. Inevitably, that Barabbas side to our personalities comes out, and we choose the Barabbas way instead of the way of Christ.

What is the answer? How do we deal with the Barabbas side to our personalities? What happened to Barabbas is the answer: Jesus died in his place.

One Memorial Day some years ago, our family went downtown to Washington, DC, to view the Memorial Day Parade. That day they were to lay to rest an "unknown soldier" from the Vietnam War. A heavy mist hung in the air, and the wind blew so hard that the water went sideways instead of falling down. We had ridden the Metro to Federal Triangle, then walked the long block to the parade route. When we got to Constitution Avenue, police officers and members of the military service lined the street as far as the eye could see. It wasn't a festive crowd, but almost every person standing on the sidewalk or sitting on the curb seemed to be there for a reason.

We finally found an opening where we could get a clearer view of the procession. We stood in front of a government office building with huge heating grates. The steady roar in the background from those heating grates muffled most of the conversation. Eventually, the parade began.

The purpose of the procession was to transport the body of that "unknown soldier" from the Capitol Rotunda to its final resting place in Arlington National Cemetery. Military marching bands played subdued, almost reverential music. Rifle contingents from the various branches of the military were also low key. Numerous high-ranking officers rode in vehicles, and others walked. Finally, a horse-drawn cart bore the casket of that unknown hero who had died in Vietnam.

As the cortege passed by, I couldn't help noticing the reactions of people in the crowd. Some bowed their heads in silent prayer. The police officers and military members saluted, and others among us put our hands over our hearts. Some stared straight ahead, and some wiped tears from their eyes. Every one of us had a lump in the throat and a sense of overwhelming gratitude. It was as if each person were saying in his or her own way, "He died for me."

Of all the people in Jerusalem on that worst of Fridays we now call Good, it was perhaps Barabbas who most understood what Jesus had done. Perhaps it was Barabbas who felt it most keenly of all—Jesus died in his place. The cross was God's answer for Barabbas, and the cross is God's answer for the Barabbas in us. Try as we might, we cannot make ourselves perfect, but thanks be to God, we don't have to. You see, given the choice of who would die and who would be saved, Jesus also chose Barabbas. Jesus died for Barabbas. Praise God, Jesus died for us too.

QUESTIONS FOR DISCUSSION/REFLECTION

1. Why did the people choose Barabbas over Jesus?
2. Why did Pilate have Jesus flogged and sent to be crucified?
3. What do you think Barabbas concluded after he was released?
4. Why did Pilate "wash his hands" of the whole matter?
5. In what sense was Jesus the King of the Jews?

CHAPTER 16

THE MOCKING BY THE SOLDIERS
Matthew 27:27-31; Mark 15:16-20

> *Then the soldiers of the governor took Jesus into the governor's headquarters, and they gathered the whole cohort around him. They stripped him and put a scarlet robe on him, and after twisting some thorns into a crown, they put it on his head. They put a reed in his right hand and knelt before him and mocked him, saying, "Hail, King of the Jews!" They spat on him, and took the reed and struck him on the head. (Matthew 27:27-30, NRSV)*

Before crucifying Jesus, the soldiers mocked him. The mocking included being stripped, clothed with a purple robe, crowned with thorns, spat on, and struck on the head. They also shouted, "Hail, King of the Jews!" and knelt down in feigned homage. The point was to humiliate Jesus and to justify in the soldiers' minds what they were about to do to him. Crucifixion was designed as a horrifying, painful, humiliating punishment. Even though Pilate had said Jesus did not deserve to die, much less to die like that, the soldiers' treatment of Jesus, including flogging him, seemed to say he did deserve it. In the noncanonical Gospel of Peter (3:9) the cruelty included others who "stood and spat in his eyes and still others [who] slapped his cheeks; others pricked him with a reed, and some of them scourged him, saying, 'With this honor let us honor the Son of God.'"

THE CRUCIFIED GOD
Matthew 27:27-31, 45-50

Jürgen was born in Hamburg, Germany, in 1926. He grew up in a secular family that had little use for religion. As a teenager, Jürgen idolized Albert Einstein, and he planned to study mathematics at the university. Jürgen passed his entrance exam, but instead he was drafted into the German army in 1944. At the age of eighteen he was sent to Reichswald, a German forest on the front lines. Jürgen surrendered in the dark to the first British soldier he met. For the next three years, he was confined to a series of prisoner-of-war camps.

Jürgen's first confinement was in Belgium. In the camp, he and the other prisoners had little to do but ruminate over the defeat of their country. Jürgen began to lose confidence in German culture because of what the Nazis had done. He and the other prisoners were forced to confront the horrors of the Holocaust. Photographs of the concentration camps at Buchenwald and Bergen-Belsen were nailed to the walls in the huts where the prisoners slept. Jürgen said his feelings of shame were so great that he often wished he had died along with his comrades rather than having to live with the guilt over the atrocities committed by his fellow Germans. There in the camp in Belgium, Jürgen met a group of Christians and was given a small New Testament by an American army chaplain. As he read the Bible and talked with the Christian believers, he felt drawn to the Christian faith. Jürgen later said, "I didn't find Christ; he found me."

After his time in the camp in Belgium, Jürgen was transferred to a POW camp in Scotland. There he and other POWs helped rebuild areas damaged by the Nazi blitzkrieg. Jürgen was greatly impressed by the kindness and hospitality of the Scottish villagers. Later that year, he was transferred to another POW camp in England, operated by the YMCA. He met some theology students there and was exposed for the first time to books of theology. The first book he read was Reinhold Niebuhr's *Nature and Destiny of Man* (originally published as two volumes in 1943), and it had a huge impact on his thinking. The book helped him to place his war experiences in a theological context. Niebuhr wrote of the reality of sin and the hope of forgiveness.

Finally, Jürgen was released and allowed to return to Germany. He found his hometown of Hamburg in ruins from the Allied bombings. Jürgen resumed his education, but instead of studying mathematics, he studied theology. His professors were followers of Karl Barth and the confessing church in Germany, which had broken away from the state church and refused to support the Nazi regime. Jürgen was also influenced by the writings of Dietrich Bonhoeffer, the German pastor and professor who had joined an unsuccessful plot against Hitler and was executed in a concentration camp near the end of the war. Jürgen received his doctorate in theology in 1952 and became pastor of an Evangelical church in Germany, where he served for the next five years. Then he became a professor of theology at an academy operated by the Confessing church. In 1967, he was appointed professor of Systematic Theology at the University of Tübingen, where he taught for the rest of his career.

Jürgen Moltmann is recognized today as one of the leading Christian theologians of the second half of the twentieth century. Among his many books are two classics in Christian thought, deeply influenced by his wartime experiences: *The Theology of Hope*, published in English in 1967, and *The Crucified God*, published in English in 1974. Moltmann's experiences as a POW helped him to formulate a

The Mocking by the Soldiers

theology of hope centered in the cross of Christ. For Jürgen Moltmann, the cross is the central revelation of God. Moltmann wrote, "At the core of Christianity we find…the God who humiliated himself…who took upon himself the suffering of inhumanity, and who died in the God-abandonedness of the cross."[1]

You cannot read the story of Jesus's suffering and death and without being appalled by the cruelty and injustice and horror of it all. They stripped him, they mocked him, they pressed a crown of thorns on his brow, they spat on him, they struck him on the head, they beat him, and, ultimately, they led him to the place of crucifixion and nailed him to a cross. There, suspended between heaven and earth, Jesus hung between two thieves as those who passed by derided him with insults and laughter. The two bandits joined in the taunts, although later one of them had a change of heart. From noon until three in the afternoon, darkness covered the whole land. Then Jesus cried with a loud voice in Hebrew, "Eli, Eli, lema sabachthani?" which means, "My God, my God, why have you forsaken me?"

Because we have heard the story before, it is not shocking to us. But it should be shocking that God allowed this to happen. God allowed the Son to suffer. God allowed Jesus to be tortured and to die an agonizing death. That should astonish us. That should amaze us. That should humble us. As Paul wrote in Romans 8:32, "He did not spare his own Son, but gave him up for us all."

When Jesus prayed, "My God, my God, why have you forsaken me?" he was expressing the anguish of abandonment that came from taking on the sins of the world. He endured excruciating physical pain, but the spiritual torment was even worse. Yet his words of anguish were also a prayer. Jesus prayed the words of the 22nd Psalm as he hung dying on the cross. Some of the bystanders did not know their scripture because they mistakenly thought he was calling on Elijah to come save him. They did not recognize that Jesus was quoting scripture even as he was dying.

Why would God allow Jesus to suffer this way? Because the cross was the only way that God could show the extent of God's love for us. Moltmann said the cross represents the suffering love of God. Jesus wasn't the only one who suffered that day. God suffered too. God suffered not because God had to suffer but because God chose to suffer. God reached out in love to take on all the sins and hurts and sufferings of the world. In the cross of Christ, God took on the sin and suffering and death of the world so we might have forgiveness and peace and life.

Eliezer was born in 1928 in a town in Romania. His parents were devout Jews who encouraged him to study the Torah and instilled in him a strong sense of humanism. In 1944, the year that Jürgen Moltmann was drafted in the German army, Eliezer and his family were arrested and deported to Auschwitz. The family was separated at the concentration camp, and Eliezer never saw his mother or younger sister again. He and his father were assigned to a work detail. In 1945, they were force marched to Buchenwald, where his father died of dysentery, starvation, and exhaustion only months before the Third Army liberated the camp.[2]

After the war, Eliezer was sent to a French orphanage. Then he studied at the Sorbonne in Paris. He taught Hebrew and served as a choirmaster to support himself, then became a journalist for a French newspaper. For ten years after the war, Eliezer refused to say anything about the Holocaust. His memories were too much for words. However, a friend finally convinced Eliezer that the best way to deal with those memories was to write about his experience. Eliezer wrote a 900-page memoir in Yiddish. Then he rewrote a shortened version in French, which was later translated into English. He moved to the United States but had trouble finding a publisher. In 1960, the English translation was published, selling just over a thousand copies. Gradually the book, simply titled *Night*, received positive reviews from literary critics. Eventually it was translated into more than thirty languages, with many millions of copies in print. After Oprah Winfrey selected the book for her book club in 2006, it became number one on the *New York Times* bestseller list for nonfiction paperbacks.

Eliezer "Elie" Wiesel became a spokesperson for Holocaust survivors and a voice of conscience speaking out against all oppression. He was awarded the Congressional Gold Medal, the Nobel Peace Prize, and the Presidential Medal of Freedom. After becoming an American citizen, he was professor of humanities at Boston University until his death in 2016.

In 1944, two teenagers, one a secular German and the other a Romanian Jew, entered their own dark nights of the soul. One was drafted into the German army; the other was deported to a concentration camp. Both young men were haunted by their memories. Both grappled with their understanding of God, and both eventually came to find hope even amid suffering.

Jürgen Moltmann wrote that he was helped by reading a particular story in Elie Wiesel's book. Two Jewish men and a child were hanged. The other prisoners were forced to watch. The men died quickly, but the boy writhed in agony for a long time. Wiesel wrote, "Then someone behind me said, 'Where is God?' and I was silent. And half an hour he cried out again, 'Where is God? Where is he?' And a voice in me answered: 'Where is God?…he hangs there on the gallows.'"[3]

In the cross of Christ, God took on all the sufferings of the world. "Amazing love! How can it be, that Thou, my God, should die for me!"[4]

QUESTIONS FOR DISCUSSION/REFLECTION

1. Why do you think the soldiers mocked and tortured Jesus?
2. Why did God allow Jesus to suffer as he did?
3. What do you think was the meaning of the scarlet robe and crown of thorns?
4. What is our hope in the death of Jesus?
5. In what sense was God crucified?

NOTES

[1] Moltmann, *The Crucified God* (Harper & Row, 1974).

[2] Note: Details about the lives of Moltmann and Wiesel are easily discovered via online searches and in their writings.

[3] Wiesel, *Night* (Bantam Books, 1982), 61–62.

[4] Charles Wesley, "And Can It Be, that I Should Gain?" 1738, https://hymnary.org/text/and_can_it_be_that_i_should_gain.

CHAPTER 17

SIMON OF CYRENE CARRIES JESUS'S CROSS
Matthew 27:32; Mark 15:21; Luke 23:26-32

They compelled a passer-by, who was coming in from the country, to carry his cross; it was Simon of Cyrene, the father of Alexander and Rufus. (Mark 15:21, NRSV)

The soldiers compelled a heretofore uninvolved passerby named Simon of Cyrene to carry Jesus's cross. Mark identifies Simon as the father of Alexander and Rufus, probably because Mark's readers knew them. Luke adds that a great number of people followed, among them women who beat their chests and wailed. Jesus told them not to weep for him but for themselves and their children. They were to weep for themselves because the days were coming when they would say, "Blessed are the barren, and the wombs that never bore, and the breasts that never nursed." They also would say to the mountains, "Fall on us," and to the hills, "Cover us." This last statement is a quotation from Hosea 10:8. A variation of the quotation also appears in Revelation 6:16. Such catastrophes are not literal but represent divine judgment on the Day of the Lord. Two criminals were also led away to be put to death with Jesus.

BURDEN INTO BLESSING
Mark 15:16-25

Years ago, I conducted a funeral for a longtime church member who passed away at an elderly age. After the funeral service at the church, I got into the lead car with the funeral director to begin the procession to the cemetery. We got on the Beltway (I-495), and the hearse and a dozen or so cars followed us. We were just reaching full speed when another funeral procession from another funeral began to enter the Beltway. Somehow or other, the last two cars from our procession got mixed up and joined the procession from the other funeral. To make matters worse, both processions headed to the same cemetery, so the drivers of the last two cars did not recognize their mistake.

When our procession arrived at the gravesite, we realized that some of the pallbearers were not with us. Then what had happened became clear. Our only recourse was to wait and hope they would realize they were with the wrong funeral. While we waited, one of the gravediggers at the cemetery discovered another error. We had been led to the wrong gravesite. Since we had arrived earlier than expected, the attendant at the cemetery had confused our procession with yet another group. Talk about being at the wrong place at the wrong time! I can only imagine the trauma to the family if we had laid their loved one to rest in the wrong burial plot.

Thankfully, the missing cars caught up with us and we moved on to the correct gravesite without the family ever knowing what had happened. But being in the wrong place at the wrong time can cause considerable grief.

Simon of Cyrene was also in the wrong place at the wrong time. It was the Passover season, and apparently Simon had come from his home in North Africa to observe Passover in Jerusalem. Perhaps he had looked forward to this pilgrimage for a long time. Maybe he had saved his money for years to make the long journey to Jerusalem for the holy festival. No doubt he wanted to celebrate Passover with other pilgrims in the great temple there. Perhaps he also looked forward to sightseeing while he was in Jerusalem, taking in some of the historic sites so important to the Jewish faith. But something happened to interrupt his plans.

Just as Simon was about to enter the city, another kind of procession came out of the city gate. It was an ugly, vile, cruel procession of condemned men on the way to crucifixion. Surely this was not what Simon had in mind when he planned his trip to Jerusalem. He had come to worship God, not to witness an execution. He had come to ascend to the temple mount and offer Passover sacrifices, not carry a wooden cross up a God-forsaken hill called Golgotha. He had come to glory in the holy city of Jerusalem, not to watch men die on a garbage heap outside the city. No, Simon of Cyrene had not bargained for this at all.

Crucifixion was a vile and ugly practice. Scholars have suggested that it was one of the cruelest and most inhumane forms of execution ever imagined. Often the condemned man was viciously whipped with leather thongs spiked with bits of metal or bone. Then, he was forced to carry his own crossbeam on a procession through the city, usually taking the longest route possible to add to the humiliation and to serve as a warning to those they passed along the way. At the site of execution, he was stripped naked, and his hands were nailed to that crossbeam. Finally, he was hoisted onto the upright beam and allowed to hang there, sometimes for hours, sometimes for days, in utter degradation.

No wonder Simon did not want any part of those proceedings. Getting involved in a crucifixion was the last thing on his mind. But he did get involved.

Palestine was an occupied territory, and any man might be ordered into Roman service for any task. So, when that Roman soldier tapped Simon on the shoulder with the flat side of his spear, Simon did not have a choice. He was in the wrong place at the wrong time, and he had to get involved.

I don't know why, but life has a way of finding us in the wrong place at the wrong time. Life has a way of laying burdens on us that we do not want, responsibilities that we did not ask for, difficult circumstances that we cannot avoid. Like Simon of Cyrene, we find ourselves where we do not want to be, and it seems there's no getting out of it. Sometimes it's not even our fault.

As a pastor, I was constantly reminded how often life takes a wrong turn, and good people are saddled with burdens they do not deserve. Illness in the family, grief over the loss of a loved one, concern for aging parents or sick children, marital stress, financial worries—it seems that everywhere we look we see people staggering under the burdens of life. Everywhere we look we see people carrying crosses they did not choose. It seems that in some ways, Simon of Cyrene is a picture of every one of us. Just when we least expect it, our plans get interrupted by some unwanted burden. We find ourselves in the wrong place at the wrong time. An unforeseen cross is laid upon us, and we have no choice but to bear it.

That kind of experience happened to me during my first year of seminary in Louisville, Kentucky. I had just completed my first semester of studies when I came down with a mysterious illness. After ten days in the hospital, they concluded that I had some kind of liver malfunction, something akin to hepatitis. It was debilitating. I spent most of the next three months flat on my back in bed. I had to drop out of school and return home to Texas to stay with my parents. Those months were the most miserable time of my life. I couldn't read without getting a headache, I couldn't go anywhere, I could only watch television in short stretches, I didn't feel like eating, I had trouble sleeping, and I sank into a deep depression. Day after day, night after night, I asked God why this was happening to me. What did I do to deserve such torment? Why had God allowed that disease to strike me down in the prime of life? After all, I was studying for the ministry! I was preparing to spend my life in God's service! Why would God lay such a burden on me?

After many prayers of anguish, there were no answers—at least none that I could understand. To this day, I cannot explain why it happened. But I do know this: I now know that God was at work in that terrible experience to bring good out of it. That, I believe, is the message of Simon of Cyrene carrying the cross of Jesus. God was at work in that terrible experience to bring good out of it.

We know virtually nothing about Simon of Cyrene except that he carried Jesus's cross and had two sons named Rufus and Alexander. But the last fact tells us a great deal. It's interesting that Mark, in writing his Gospel, identifies Simon of Cyrene as the father of Rufus and Alexander. Matthew and Luke tell us about Simon, but they do not mention his sons. Why would Mark give their names? It is likely that Mark identified Simon that way because Rufus and Alexander were known to his readers. Maybe they were well-known members of Mark's church. Paul's letter to the Romans mentions a church worker named Rufus, and perhaps he was the same person (Rom 16:13). Rufus and Alexander must have been prominent early Christian leaders, and Mark says their father carried Jesus's cross. Can we read between the lines? How did Rufus and Alexander become Christians? Did their father Simon lead the way?

The Gospel of Mark was written around AD 60 or 70, according to most biblical scholars. That was thirty or forty years after Jesus's death. Probably Simon had died by then, but his sons Rufus and Alexander were still part of the church. It is not unreasonable to think that their father led them to Christ. It is not unreasonable to think that Simon, after he carried the cross, became a follower of Jesus himself. I can imagine Simon telling his sons the story of bearing the cross of Christ and describing how his life changed from that moment on. A burden became a blessing. What began as an agonizing experience for Simon became the means by which he came to know Jesus as his Savior.

That can happen for us. I don't suggest that every illness, every problem, every loss, or every burden is God's design. But I do affirm that God can use those burdens. God can transform those crosses to bring blessings out of them. That happened for me. I never want to go through a debilitating illness again. It actually took five or six years for me to begin to feel really well. Even so, God did bring good out of it. Because I was so sick myself, I now have deeper sympathy for people who suffer. Because I was sick for so long, I now have deeper gratitude for life and deeper appreciation for health. Because of that illness, I have deeper awareness of the preciousness of life and the problems of suffering. Because of that illness, I learned things I might not learn any other way. God brought blessing out of burden for Simon, and God brought blessing out of burden for me. God can do it for you too.

I don't want to trivialize any burden you may be carrying. I don't want to suggest that as long as you have faith, everything will work out the way you want it to. Sometimes that doesn't happen. Sometimes loved ones die, sometimes illness comes, sometimes bad things happen to us that we do not deserve, and sometimes tragedy appears without warning. But if the gospel tells us anything—if Jesus dying on the cross tells us anything—it is that God can bring good even out of that.

I debated whether I should share about the mistakes at the funeral. I feared it might sound insensitive, like I was joking about it. Funerals are not joking matters. We never want to make light of suffering and heartache and death.

But in a profound sense, because of what happened to Jesus, we can see death in a new way. Because Jesus rose from the grave, death is not the last word to life. Out of the pain and agony and utter indignity of the cross, God brought forth a new and glorious and everlasting life. When Jesus rose from the grave, it was as if God pulled the biggest joke of all. It was as if God said to death, "Oh no, you don't! I've got the last laugh, death. The joke is on you."

Centuries ago, an unusual custom developed in the Greek Orthodox church. On the day after Easter, the pastor and people would gather in the church to tell amusing anecdotes, funny stories, jokes. What better way, they thought, to celebrate the resurrection than with lightheartedness and laughter and frivolity and joy? So they laughed until they cried, and they celebrated God's victory over death with the biggest party we can imagine.

This is the answer to every cross. If God could bring good out of the cross on Golgotha, God can bring good out of any cross we might bear. Yes, we can joke, we can laugh, and we can rejoice. In the end, even death cannot defeat us, for our God gives us reasons for joy, even in the midst of tears.

QUESTIONS FOR DISCUSSION/REFLECTION

1. Can you picture yourself in Simon of Cyrene's place?
2. Why did the soldiers compel Simon to carry Jesus's cross?
3. How do you think that experience affected Simon?
4. In what sense might we carry Jesus's cross?
5. How has God turned a burden into a blessing in your life?

CHAPTER 18

THE CRUCIFIXION
Matthew 27:33-44; Mark 15:22-32; Luke 23:33-43

Then he said, "Jesus, remember me when you come into your kingdom." He replied, "Truly I tell you, today you will be with me in Paradise." (Luke 23:42-43, NRSV)

The site of crucifixion was Golgotha, the place of the skull. The soldiers crucified Jesus between two criminals. They offered him wine to drink, perhaps as a kind of sedative or perhaps to taunt him, but he wouldn't take it. Jesus prayed, "Father, forgive them; for they do not know what they are doing" (Luke 23:34). They divided his clothing among themselves, casting lots. It was nine o'clock in the morning, and people stood by watching. An inscription was placed over his head with the charge against him, "The King of the Jews" (Mark 15:26). Passersby derided him. Some said, "You who would destroy the temple and build it in three days, save yourself, and come down from the cross!" (Mark 15:29-30). The chief priests, scribes, and elders also mocked him, saying, "He saved others; he cannot save himself. Let the Messiah, the King of Israel, come down from the cross now, so that we may see and believe" (Mark 15:31-32). The bandits crucified alongside him joined in taunting him. The soldiers also mocked him. One of the criminals kept deriding him, but the other criminal heard enough and had a change of heart. He said, "We have been justly condemned…but this man has done nothing wrong" (Luke 23:41). He asked Jesus to remember him when he came into his kingdom. Jesus replied, "Today you will be with me in Paradise" (Luke 23:43).

WITH ME IN PARADISE
Luke 23:32-43

After our friends Don and Norma Harris retired and moved to Florida, we began to visit them every winter. We usually went for four or five days, or for a week if we planned to visit other friends. Don and Norma had a beautiful condo in Fort Myers overlooking a golf course in a gated community. It was a delightful place to get away. The weather was usually ideal, and there was plenty to see and do. In addition to playing golf, we went sightseeing. We went to Estero and Sanibel and Captiva islands. We took a dolphin cruise. We toured the Ding Darling National Wildlife Refuge. We visited the Edison-Ford Winter Estates.

Thomas Edison first visited Fort Myers in the winter of 1885. He was so entranced by the climate and natural beauty that he bought property there and established a winter residence. Henry Ford visited Edison at his winter home, and he was so taken with Fort Myers that he built a winter home right next to Edison's house. Both homes were restored and are now the centerpieces of a twenty-acre museum.

The city of Fort Myers takes understandable pride in the fact that Thomas Edison and Henry Ford chose to spend part of their winters there. The Edison-Ford Estate is a major attraction, drawing more than 250,000 visitors a year. Set on the Caloosahatchee River just south of downtown Fort Myers, the site's picturesque view must have provided many enjoyable times for Thomas Edison and Henry Ford and their families.

On our first visit to Fort Myers, we were surprised to hear several people welcome us to "paradise." We came to find out that the locals are not shy about calling their city "paradise." With an average yearly temperature of seventy-five degrees and breezes blowing inland from the Gulf, the weather is mild in the winter and not too unbearably hot in the summer (or so they say). The local Chamber of Commerce boasts that the sun shines almost every day of the year.

So there are many things to do in Fort Myers. Besides golf, there's tennis, beaches, fishing and boating, birdwatching, biking, and hiking. The area offers breathtaking sunsets and a casual, laid-back lifestyle. Some people wear shorts just about every day. You can understand why some immodestly call it "paradise."

A lot of businesses in and around Fort Myers have picked up on the paradise theme. There's Paradise Bar and Grill, Paradise Resort, Paradise Luxury Condos, Paradise Boat Rentals, Paradise Golf Academy, Paradise Hauling, Paradise Parasail, and even Paradise Adult Day Care Center. Apparently, many people in Fort Myers think they really are living in paradise (except when a hurricane blows through).

Jesus said to the penitent dying thief on the cross, "Today you will be with me in Paradise" (Luke 23:43). What did Jesus mean?

Our English word "paradise" comes from the Latin word *paradises*, which came from the Greek word *paradeisos*, which came from the Persian word *pairi-daeza*. Paradise was not a Jewish term but a borrowed word from the ancient Persians. The Persians used the word to refer to an enclosure or a park or a garden. When the Old Testament was translated from Hebrew into Greek, known as the Septuagint, the Greek word for "paradise" was used for the Garden of Eden in the book of Genesis.

In Genesis 2,

> ...the LORD God formed man from the dust of the ground, and breathed into his nostrils the breath of life; and the man became a living being. And the LORD God planted a garden in Eden, in the east; and there he put the man whom he had formed. Out of the ground the LORD God made to grow every tree that is pleasant to the sight and good for food, the tree of life also in the midst of the garden, and the tree of the knowledge of good and evil....
>
> The LORD God took the man and put him in the garden of Eden to till it and keep it. And the LORD God commanded the man, "You may freely eat of every tree of the garden; but of the tree of the knowledge of good and evil you shall not eat, for in the day that you eat of it you shall die."
>
> Then the LORD God said, "It is not good that the man should be alone; I will make him a helper as his partner." So out of the ground the LORD God formed every animal of the field and every bird of the air, and brought them to the man to see what he would call them; and whatever the man called each living creature, that was its name. The man gave names to...[every living creature]; but for the man there was not found a helper as his partner. So the LORD God caused a deep sleep to fall upon the man, and he slept; then he took one of his ribs and closed up its place with flesh. And the rib that the LORD God had taken from the man he made into a woman and brought her to the man. Then the man said, "This at last is bone of my bones and flesh of my flesh; this one shall be called Woman, for out of Man this one was taken." Therefore a man leaves his father and his mother and clings to his wife, and they become one flesh. And the man and his wife were both na-ked, and were not ashamed. (vv. 7-9, 15-25)

The story of creation in the book of Genesis describes God's intent for creation. God created a human out of the dust of the ground and blew into his lungs the breath of life, and the human became a living being. God placed him in a garden expressly designed for his well-being. God provided the human everything he needed to prosper—food and water, other living creatures, meaningful work to do in managing the garden, and finally a helper to be his partner, the woman who became his wife. Everything was there not just for the humans to survive but to thrive.

The garden was a place free from trouble. It was a place where the man and woman lived in harmony with one another and with nature (hence there was not even the need for clothing). It was a place where the man and woman lived in communion with God. It was a place free from death. But it was not a place free from temptation. When the man and woman disobeyed God and ate from the tree of the knowledge of good and evil, they were banned from the Garden of Eden and cast out of Paradise. In a sense, the human longing is to return to Paradise.

In the time of Jesus, that was the Jewish hope—to return to Paradise. The Jews did not yet have a strong concept of heaven, although some Jews like the Pharisees believed in the resurrection of the righteous to life after death. But all Jews longed for a return to Paradise, and they believed the Messiah would open the way for them to return to the garden of harmony and beauty and peace. Isaiah prophesied that Zion would become like Eden when the Messiah came, and harmony would once again be restored (Isaiah 51:3). The Jews did not fully understand about heaven, for only after the resurrection of Jesus did life after death become a certain hope. But they did hope to return to Paradise, which the early Christians naturally associated with heaven.

Two thieves were crucified alongside Jesus, one on his right and one on his left. Matthew and Mark say those thieves joined in taunting Jesus, along with those who jeered as they passed by. But only Luke tells us that one of the thieves had second thoughts as he hung there dying on the cross. The penitent thief had a change of heart. He said to his fellow thief, "Don't you fear God? We have been justly condemned and we are getting exactly what we deserve, but this man has done nothing wrong" (Luke 23:40-41, my paraphrase). The penitent thief acknowledged his crimes, admitted his guilt, and confessed his sin. Then he said to Jesus, "Remember me when you come into your kingdom" (v. 42). What an astonishing thing to say to another man dying on a cross! What kind of kingdom could a dead man possibly receive? Yet this penitent thief had a faith that went beyond the present circumstances, and Jesus promised him more than he asked for. The man had asked for a place in Jesus's kingdom, and Jesus promised that the dying man would be with him in Paradise.

In some way, we are all looking for Paradise. We are all looking for a place of contentment and peace. What is paradise for you? For some people, it is having all the money they could want. For others, it is a loving family or perfect health or a deeply fulfilling job. For others, it is retiring and moving to Florida—Fort Myers even! But in our heart of hearts, we know that Paradise is more than that. Paradise is communion with God. Paradise is partnership with other human beings. Paradise is harmony with nature. Paradise is returning to that state of bliss where there is no more sorrow, no more trouble, even no more death. Paradise, in the words of the apostle Paul, is "to be with the Lord forever" (1 Thess 4:17).

When Adam and Eve sinned against God, they were cast out of the Garden of Eden and cut off from the tree of life. No longer were they protected from

The Crucifixion

death, for the tree of life in the midst of Paradise was beyond their reach. But when Jesus died on the cross, his tree of death became the tree of life for those who place their faith in him. Prudentius, the fourth century Roman Christian poet, said to enter Paradise is to return to "our native country." Human history began in a Garden, and human history must end in a Garden if we are ever to find our way home. Paradise is our origin, and Paradise is our ultimate destination as well. It is a place of harmony and peace and communion. It is a place where we can live forever with our Lord. "Today you will be with me in Paradise," Jesus said. Today…today…today!

QUESTIONS FOR DISCUSSION/REFLECTION

1. Why did the thieves who were being crucified taunt Jesus?
2. Why do you think the one thief had a change of heart?
3. What is Paradise to you?
4. In what sense can we be with Jesus in Paradise?
5. What meaning does the death of Jesus have for you?

CHAPTER 19

THE DEATH ON THE CROSS
Matthew 27:45-56; Mark 15:33-41; Luke 23:44-49

And about three o'clock Jesus cried with a loud voice, "Eli, Eli, lema sabachthani?" that is, "My God, my God, why have you forsaken me? (Matthew 27:46, NRSV)

From noon until three in the afternoon, as Jesus hung on the cross, darkness came over the whole land. According to the noncanonical Gospel of Peter, "the sun had set while Jesus was still alive" (5:15). Matthew, Mark, and Luke say that "the curtain of the temple was torn in two" (Luke 23:45). Matthew and Mark record Jesus's cry, "Eli, Eli, lema sabachthani," a quotation from Psalm 22:1. Some bystanders thought Jesus was calling for Elijah to save him. Luke adds Jesus's final words: "Father, into your hands I commend my Spirit" (Luke 23:46). Matthew adds that the earth shook, tombs opened, and the bodies of many saints were raised. The centurion keeping watch over Jesus saw the earthquake and reacted. Luke said he praised God and said, "Certainly this man was innocent" (Luke 23:47). Matthew (27:54) and Mark (15:39) quoted the centurion as saying, "Truly this man was God's Son!" Women who had followed Jesus from Galilee were also there, including Mary Magdalene, Mary the mother of James and Joseph, the mother of the sons of Zebedee, and Salome. John adds that standing near the cross were "his mother, and his mother's sister, Mary the wife of Clopas," and John himself (John 19:25). So Jesus did not die alone.

FORSAKEN?
Matthew 27:45-50

Together, Matthew, Mark, Luke, and John record seven statements Jesus spoke from the cross. John records three of them, Luke records three of them, and Matthew and Mark give us just this one: "My God, my God, why have you forsaken me?" According to Mark, Jesus was crucified at the third hour on Friday morning, meaning 9:00 a.m. At the sixth hour, meaning at noontime, the sky went dark. For three more hours, until 3:00 p.m., Jesus hung on the cross in darkness. Finally, after six hours on the cross, Jesus died.

It is possible that Jesus said more than seven statements. Even though he was in torment, Jesus was conscious. Suspended only a few feet above the ground, Jesus may have talked with the women, with his beloved disciple John, with the soldiers standing guard, or with the thieves crucified alongside him. In fact, we know that Jesus talked with some of them, for his words to them are included in the seven statements recorded in the four Gospels.

John remembered three of those statements. After all, John was there, at least for part of the time. According to John, Jesus said to his mother, "Woman, here is your son" (19:26), and to the disciple he said, "Here is your mother" (v. 27). Also, according to John, Jesus said, "I am thirsty" (v. 28), and then he said, "It is finished" (v. 30). Those are the three statements from Jesus on the cross in John's Gospel.

Luke records three other statements that Jesus said from the cross. As far as we know, Luke was not there. Some scholars believe he used Mary, Jesus's mother who was there, as his primary source. As a careful historian, Luke probably interviewed all the eyewitnesses he could locate. And Luke's sources gave him three other statements from the lips of Jesus as he was dying on the cross. According to Luke, Jesus said, "Father, forgive them; for they know not what they are doing" (23:34). Luke also records two other statements: "Today you will be with me in Paradise" (v. 43), and "Father, into your hands I commend my spirit" (v. 46).

Matthew and Mark tell us none of those statements. In Matthew and Mark, the only thing Jesus says from the cross is this shattering statement: "My God, my God, why have you forsaken me?"

As far as we know, Matthew and Mark were not there at the foot of the cross. Matthew was one of the twelve disciples, but we know that except for John, the rest of them ran away and hid when Jesus died. Mark was probably too young to be a disciple, but later he did become one of the leaders of the early church. Reliable traditions tell us that Mark became a close confidant of the apostle Simon Peter, and it is likely that Mark got much of his information for his Gospel from Peter. But, of course, Peter was not at the foot of the cross either. How strange that Matthew and Mark should only record this statement in their accounts of Jesus on the cross.

The Gospels are not histories in the classic sense of the term. They contain historical information, but they do not purport to present it in an unbiased fashion. Matthew, Mark, Luke, and John all acknowledge their biases from the beginning. All four writers were convinced that Jesus was the Christ, the Son of God, and they constructed their Gospels to prove that point. They were all deliberately selective in choosing what information to include. They realized they were not telling everything about Jesus. John, in the very last verse of his Gospel, wrote, "But there are also many other things that Jesus did; if every one of them were written down, I suppose that the world itself could not contain the books that would be written" (21:25).

Since the Gospel writers could not include everything they knew about Jesus, they included only what they considered most important. John considered it important that we know Jesus entrusted the care of his mother and the beloved disciple to one another. He considered it important that we know Jesus said, "I am thirsty" and "It is finished!" Luke considered it important that we know Jesus prayed for forgiveness for those who had hurt him. He considered it important that we know what Jesus said to the penitent thief on the cross and that Jesus said, "Father, into your hands I commend my spirit."

Matthew and Mark wanted us to know that Jesus said something else. Theologians have called it the "cry of dereliction." It's a direct quotation from Psalm 22, which begins, "My God, my God, why have you forsaken me?" We should not be surprised that Jesus quoted scripture from the cross. He knew the scriptures. It is not surprising that he quoted from the holy writings in his hour of need. But why this scripture? Why Psalm 22? Why not a more tranquil passage, like the 23rd Psalm, "The LORD is my Shepherd, I shall not want" (v. 1)? Why not Psalm 27: "The LORD is my light and my salvation; whom shall I fear" (v. 1)? Why not Psalm 40: "I waited patiently for the LORD; he inclined to me and heard my cry" (v. 1)? Why not some other verse of peace and consolation? Of all the verses Jesus could have quoted, this is perhaps the most disturbing. Did Jesus really feel that God had forsaken him?

It is true that just about everybody had forsaken him. Only John and a few women stood beside him as he hung on the cross. Everyone else had turned their backs on him. Judas had betrayed him. Peter had denied him. The others had run out on him. But had God run out on him? Did Jesus believe that God had abandoned him in his time of greatest crisis?

We can never know for sure what Jesus felt. My intuition is that Jesus probably did feel abandoned by God at that point. There are times in every life when we wonder where God is in the midst of trouble. As a pastor, I had the holy privilege, and the holy burden, of being with people in their darkest hours. I was there when the surgeon came out after the operation and told the family that the cancer had spread and there was nothing more they could do. I've been there with loved ones in the aftermath of suicide or following a traffic accident when a young life was taken far too soon. I've been there after a wife comes home and finds a note from her husband on the kitchen table saying he is leaving her. I've been there after a highly respected professional got word that his job was about to be terminated. I've been there when dark family secrets have come out. There are times in every life when we wonder where God is. There are times when life seems so dark and we feel so alone that we wonder if God has forsaken us.

I read an article about the late actor Burt Reynolds in *Parade Magazine* that shared something I had not known (March 8, 1992). I did not know until I read the article that Burt Reynolds spent two years of his life in his own private hell suffering from effects of a head injury. In 1984, he was struck with a chair while filming a movie, and the blow crushed his jaw joint. That in turn crushed the eustachian tubes in his ears and destroyed his sense of balance. For two years, he couldn't stand up, chew food, or endure many lights or sounds. He spent most of those two years lying in bed in a dark room in his home. His weight dropped from 200 pounds to 138 pounds. The doctors told him there was nothing they could do and that he would never leave his bed again except in a wheelchair. To make matters worse, people began to spread rumors about him. They questioned his sexual orientation. They said he had AIDS. Comedians joked about it. "I was incredibly hurt," Reynolds said, "but what amazed me were the friends who abandoned us."

It can happen to anybody—that feeling of abandonment. Sometimes we can feel so alone that we wonder if God has abandoned us too. I think that may be why Matthew and Mark recorded this one statement from Jesus on the cross. They wanted us to know that Jesus went through that kind of experience. They wanted us to know that Jesus felt abandoned and forsaken. That means Jesus knows where we're coming from. Jesus understands how we feel. Jesus identifies with our fears and our failings and our disappointments. Jesus sympathizes with what it is like to feel rejected and run out on. Jesus has been there. That doesn't automatically make everything all right, but it helps to know that Somebody understands.

During those two years of his personal torment, Burt Reynolds said that while most of his friends deserted him, a few people remained faithful. One person who called him every week to see how he was doing was *Tonight Show* host Johnny Carson. Another person who never left his side was his wife, Loni Anderson. Somehow, knowing that he was not alone, Burt found the strength to begin the long journey back to health. Even though it was excruciating for him to even get out of bed, he went to more than thirty oral surgeons until he found one who could repair his jaw. Finally, he found an ear specialist who could fix his crushed eustachian tubes to restore his balance and cure his constant nausea. Gradually, he was able to gain his weight back. Little by little, with the help and encouragement of those who really cared about him, he began to make his way back. He said, "Loni and I pray together every night, and it's mainly to thank the Lord that we made it through."

If the story of Jesus ended with the word of forsakenness, we would conclude that God did forsake Jesus. But this was not the last word. Even though he felt terribly alone, Jesus was still able to pray, "My God, my God...." If Jesus had addressed his cry of anguish to the crowd, "Why has God forsaken me?" we might conclude that he really was abandoned. But Jesus addressed his cry of anguish to God. Even in his cry of desolation, Jesus knew that God had not run out on him. The fact that Jesus prayed to God meant he knew God was there for him. God was there amid the pain and the darkness, the heartache and the loneliness. God was there for Jesus, and God is there for us.

Georgia Harkness wrote, "The cross is God's way of uniting suffering with love."[1] This is the staggering truth of the cross: only in the midst of suffering is the love of God most clearly manifest. As someone said, it is only when it gets dark enough that you can see the stars.

Did Jesus feel forsaken? Yes, for a time he probably did. But did God run out on Jesus? Never. For just when God seems farthest off, God is in our hearts and nearest to us.

What do we do when we feel forsaken? We do as Jesus did—we pray. We pray even if the only prayer we can utter is our feelings of abandonment. We pray, and we keep on, certain that somehow and some way the Lord will see us through.

QUESTIONS FOR DISCUSSION/REFLECTION

1. Why do you think Jesus prayed, "My God, my God, why have you forsaken me?"
2. Do you think Jesus really felt forsaken by God?
3. Have there been times in your life when you felt forsaken?
4. What can we do when life seems to turn against us?
5. Why did God not deliver Jesus from the cross?

NOTE

[1]Georgia Harkness, *The Modern Rival of Christian Faith* (New York: Abingdon-Cokesbury Press, 1952).

CHAPTER 20

THE BURIAL OF JESUS
Matthew 27:57-61; Mark 15:42-47; Luke 23:50-56

Now there was a good and righteous man named Joseph, who, though a member of the council, had not agreed to their plan and action. He came from the Jewish town of Arimathea, and he was waiting expectantly for the kingdom of God. This man went to Pilate and asked for the body of Jesus. (Luke 23:50-52, NRSV)

His name was Joseph, and he was originally from the Jewish town of Arimathea. He was a rich and respected member of the council. Because he was a secret disciple of Jesus, he had not agreed with the plan to have Jesus killed. Joseph of Arimathea went to Pilate and asked for Jesus's body. With Pilate's permission, Joseph bought a linen cloth, took Jesus down from the cross, wrapped his body in the cloth, and laid it in his own new rock-hewn tomb. Joseph had to hurry because the Sabbath was fast approaching. He rolled a great stone against the tomb opening and went away. The women who had followed Jesus from Galilee, including Mary Magdalene and Mary the mother of Joses, saw where Jesus's body was laid. Seeing that the burial was performed so hastily, they went back to where they were staying and prepared ointments and spices. Their intent was to give Jesus's body a proper burial. They would return after the Sabbath was over, because they obeyed the commandment to rest.

JOSEPH OF ARIMATHEA
Luke 23:50-56

Joseph of Arimathea was both a friend of Pilate and a (secret) friend of Jesus. As a member of the Jewish council, he had to hide his allegiance to Jesus. He did not agree with the council's accusations and plot against Jesus, but he was clearly outnumbered, and it would have done no good to argue on Jesus's behalf.

In most cases, the Romans did not allow families or supporters to claim the bodies of executed criminals. The corpses of the crucified were usually cast into an open pit, an unmarked mass grave. Sometimes the dead bodies were thrown onto the burning garbage heap of Gehenna, adding to the horror and indignity of crucifixion. But in this case, Joseph, a prominent Jewish leader originally from Arimathea and a member of the Sanhedrin, went to Pilate to ask permission to give Jesus a decent burial. Luke says Joseph was a good and righteous man, and Matthew says he was a disciple of Jesus. John clarifies that Joseph was a secret disciple of Jesus because of his fear of the Jews (John 19:38). John also adds that Nicodemus, who had first come to Jesus by night, joined Joseph in anointing the body with spices before they wrapped it in linen cloths. So Joseph took Jesus's body down from the cross and (with Nicodemus) anointed it with spices, wrapped it in linen, and laid it in a rock-hewn tomb where no one else had ever been buried.

The women from Galilee, who had followed Jesus to Jerusalem and seen him die, now followed the sad procession to the tomb. While most of the disciples had fled and gone into hiding after Jesus's arrest, the women never left him. Some of them had been his financial backers, providing support for Jesus and his disciples as they traveled from place to place. Now, they remained with Jesus even after his death.

Darkness descended as the stone was rolled to seal the tomb's entrance. Realizing they could do nothing more, the women went back to where they were staying in Jerusalem. They would rest on Saturday, the Sabbath, and then return early on Sunday morning to anoint the body with fragrant spices and ointments and to say goodbye for the last time to their beloved master and friend.

The burial of Jesus was enacted by brave people. Joseph was brave to ask Pilate for the body of Jesus, and Nicodemus was brave to join him in anointing the body and wrapping it in linen cloths. The women were brave to follow Jesus all the way to the cross, to watch him die, and then to follow the simple procession to the tomb. They all put themselves at risk by identifying with Jesus in such public ways. But they loved him, and they followed him, even if in secret (as with Joseph of Arimathea and Nicodemus).

Following Jesus requires bravery. Sometimes there is a risk to following Jesus. For example, Christians in the American South before and during the Civil War took a risk if they stood against slavery. In the introduction to my book *Spelunking Scripture: The Letters of Paul*,[1] I note how the Bible was used for hundreds of years to justify slavery. On page vi I begin, "As a two-time graduate of the Southern Baptist Theological Seminary, I was dismayed to learn that two founding faculty members of the seminary, John A. Broadus and James P. Boyce, were slaveowners." Like many Southern preachers and church members of their era, they found support for slavery in certain selected verses of scripture.

Yet not all Christians in the South supported slavery. I've learned about Quakers living in Alexandria, Virginia, before the Civil War who were anti-slav-

The Burial of Jesus

ery and engaged in the practice of renting and in some cases selling houses to free African Americans. Two of those Quakers were Mordecai Miller and his son Robert H. Miller.

According to articles on the City of Alexandria, Virginia, website, Mordecai Miller helped create the first free African American neighborhood in the city and was involved in the emancipation of Black slaves.[2] Mordecai built a series of houses on the 400 block of South Royal Street and rented them to free Black families. His son Robert also built houses on South Royal Street and eventually began selling those properties to Black homeowners. One researcher concluded, "under Mordecai, the community of free black renters was established, and under Robert, in 1834, it advanced toward a community of homeowners."[3] Between 1815 and 1861, free Black households occupied most of the residences on this block of South Royal Street.

In 1820, Hannah Jackson, a free Black laundress, purchased a house from Mordecai Miller, making her one of the earliest Black residents and Black women in Alexandria to own property. Jackson went on to purchase and emancipate family members, including her son and her sister and her sister's four children.

So following Jesus led some in the South, like Mordecai and Robert Miller, to defy the culture that practiced the enslavement of African Americans and submitted them to inferior status in Southern society. Guided by their anti-slavery beliefs, they helped some Black residents achieve home ownership and helped other African Americans achieve freedom from slavery. Today we laud such figures as Mordecai and Robert Miller, but in their time being anti-slavery was risky business.

It was risky business for Joseph of Arimathea to follow Jesus. Because of that, he was a secret disciple until Jesus died on the cross. By taking responsibility for the burial of Jesus's body, Joseph of Arimathea began to make his allegiance known. Along with Nicodemus, and with the women, Joseph and these followers of Jesus dared to publicly identify with the One the Romans had crucified.

In Acts 12 we read that the followers of Jesus began to pay a terrible price for their faith. James, the brother of John, a member of the inner circle of disciples closest to Jesus, was the first of the original twelve to be martyred. He was killed by the sword, presumably beheaded, under orders of King Herod Agrippa, the grandson of Herod the Great. Another of the inner circle of disciples, Peter, was arrested and imprisoned by King Herod, and many other Christians were persecuted as well. In fact, according to early church traditions, all the remaining original disciples, with the possible exception of John, died martyrs' deaths. A strong early church tradition says that Peter was crucified upside down, probably by order of the Roman Emperor Nero. There are traditions that describe the martyrdom of the other disciples too. Following Jesus was risky business indeed.

Yet the disciples were willing to die for their faith because they knew who Jesus really was.

QUESTIONS FOR DISCUSSION/REFLECTION

1. Why did Joseph of Arimathea ask Pilate for the body of Jesus?
2. What kinds of risks did burying Jesus's body have for Joseph?
3. Why did the women want to come back to the tomb on Sunday?
4. What kinds of risks do we face today in following Jesus?
5. Have there been times when following Jesus was risky business for you?

NOTES

[1] Published by Nurturing Faith, 2021.
[2] See "Historic Alexandria," *City of Alexandria Virginia*, updated June 21, 2024, alexandriava.gov/historic.
[3] T. B. McCord Jr., *Across the Fence but a World Apart* (Alexandria, VA: Alexandria Urban Archaeology Program, 1985), 25–26.

CHAPTER 21

THE GUARD AT THE TOMB
Matthew 27:62-66

The next day, that is, after the day of Preparation, the chief priests and the Pharisees gathered before Pilate and said, "Sir, we remember what that impostor said while he was still alive, 'After three days I will rise again.' Therefore command the tomb to be made secure until the third day; otherwise his disciples may go and steal him away, and tell the people, 'He has been raised from the dead,' and the last deception would be worse than the first." (Matthew 27:62-64, NRSV)

What irony! The chief priests were not afraid that Jesus would rise again. They were afraid that the disciples would steal his body and tell people that he was raised from the dead. So they asked Pilate to provide a guard of soldiers at the tomb. They thought the guard and the sealing stone would make the tomb secure. Another irony—the day of Preparation was the day before the Sabbath (Mark 15:42). That means the super-observant chief priests and Pharisees went to Pilate the next day, after the day of Preparation, which was the Sabbath. They did business on the Sabbath! Talk about hypocrisy.

THE LAST DECEPTION
Matthew 27:62-66

The movie *The Full Monty* is about six laid-off steelworkers in the city of Sheffield in northern England.[1] One character, a former foreman, cannot bring himself to tell even his own wife that he has been out of work for six months. Every morning, she packs him a lunch, and every night he comes home and tells her what went on that day at the mill. The deception is killing him. He laments to a friend, "She's out on High Street right now, with her Mastercard." His shame about being out of work and his fear of never finding another job have made his life a lie. He knows he can't go on like this, but he doesn't know what else to do. It's bad enough that he can't admit it to his wife; it's even worse that he can't admit it to himself.

The theme for Matthew 27 is deception. Jesus had died on the cross; there was no deception about that. Everyone knew he was dead—the Romans, the Jewish authorities, the women who stayed with him to the very end, his disciples who ran away. They all knew Jesus was dead and buried. But the Jewish authorities feared that his disciples would try to do something to deceive the people. They feared his disciples would break into the tomb, steal his body, and then claim that Jesus was raised from the dead.

To prevent the possibility of such a deception, the Jewish leaders went to the Roman governor, Pontius Pilate, and asked him to provide a guard of soldiers to secure the tomb where Jesus was laid. That would do two things. First, it would provide a physical deterrence to would-be grave robbers. No one would dare to challenge Roman soldiers. Second, it would provide a legal deterrence. The tomb would not only be guarded but also secured with the official seal of the Roman governor. The sealing of the tomb was kind of like sealing a letter with wax and stamping the official Roman governor's emblem in the wax. This was on a much larger scale, with the tomb sealed with some sort of malleable clay and the governor's imperial imprint pressed into the clay, but it had the same effect. Breaking the seal would be a crime, an illegal act, subject to punishment by the Roman government. Pilate granted their request. The tomb would be sealed, and a guard would be posted for three days.

The chief priests and Pharisees reported to Pilate that Jesus had said, "After three days I will rise again." But nobody really believed it—not the chief priests and Pharisees, not Pilate, and not even Jesus's own disciples. Nobody really believed that Jesus would rise again. Jesus was dead and buried. The Jewish authorities had orchestrated his execution through a smear campaign of lies and false accusations. But they still worried it was not enough.

Our Christian faith is based on the belief that Jesus rose from the dead. We believe that Jesus, who died on the cross, did not stay dead. We believe that the tomb was empty not because someone stole the body but because God raised Jesus to new life from the grave. Most importantly, we believe that Jesus is alive even now.

Admittedly, to our modern scientific minds, that is hard to explain. It's a lot easier for people today to believe that someone stole the body of Jesus from the tomb than it is to believe Jesus was resurrected from the dead never to die again. But the Bible makes it clear that the disciples did not steal the body of Jesus. That was a lie. It was a conspiracy of deception intended to hide the truth. It was a desperate, albeit illogical, attempt by the people who had killed Jesus to deny his resurrection.

How do we know that Jesus rose from the dead? How do we know that Jesus is alive even today? Like the first disciples, we know it because of our personal experiences with the risen Christ. I'm not talking about the physical appearances the disciples experienced. I've never seen the risen Jesus face to face in the way they did. But I have experienced the presence of Jesus in other ways. Let me suggest three ways that we can experience the risen Jesus in our world today.

First, we can experience the presence of the risen Jesus in the church. Jesus himself said, "where two or three are gathered in my name, I am there among them" (Matt 18:20). Yes, we can experience the risen Jesus in church. I have felt the Spirit of Christ many times in worship. I don't know that I would call it a mystical experience, but coming together with other Christians in worship makes the risen Christ available in a way that may not happen during most other moments of our lives.

Second, we can experience the presence of the risen Christ through ministry to people in need. Jesus said as we minister to the poor, the sick, and the hurting, we minister to him (Matt 25:40). One of the best ways to encounter the risen Christ is to help other people.

Third, we can experience the presence of the risen Christ in our own hearts. When we accept Jesus as our Savior and Lord, we invite him into our lives. In several of his letters Paul wrote about Christ living in the hearts of his believers. For example,

> You are no longer ruled by your desires, but by God's Spirit, who lives in you. People who don't have the Spirit of Christ in them don't belong to him. But Christ lives in you. (Rom 8:9-10, CEV)

> Christ will live in your hearts because of your faith. (Eph 3:17, CEV)

> And the mystery is that Christ lives in you, and he is your hope of sharing in God's glory. (Col 1:27, CEV)

We experience the presence of the risen Christ in our hearts when we accept Jesus as our Savior and Lord.

So we can experience the presence of the risen Christ in three ways—in the church with other Christians, in people in need whom we help, and in our hearts. The tomb was empty because Jesus was raised. Jesus is alive. Jesus Christ is with us, even today.

Every morning a young pastor noticed an older gentleman working in his garden. Invariably, the older man whistled while he worked. One day the young pastor stopped to introduce himself to the older man and to ask him about his whistling. The older man pointed to an elderly woman sitting on the porch in a wheelchair. The young pastor had never noticed her before. "That's my wife," the older gentleman explained. "She can't walk, and she can't see too well. So every time I come out to work in the garden, I roll her out on the porch so she can enjoy the fresh air. That's why I whistle; I whistle for her. When she hears my whistle, she knows that I'm close by, and she's not alone."

We cannot see Christ as he works in the garden of our lives, but if we will listen, we can hear the soft whistling of his Spirit; we can know that he is close by, and we are not alone. Jesus died and was buried. But now the tomb is empty. The world is full. Hallelujah, what a Savior!

QUESTIONS FOR DISCUSSION/REFLECTION

1. Why did the Jewish authorities ask Pilate for a guard at the tomb?
2. What kind of deception were the authorities trying to avoid?
3. What kind of deception did the authorities engage in themselves?
4. Are you surprised that no one expected Jesus to rise from the dead?
5. How is the risen Christ present in your life?

NOTE

[1] Dir. Peter Cattaneo, 20th Century Studios/Searchlight Pictures, 1997.

ADDENDUM

THE PASSION STORY IN JOHN
John 13-19

> *But there are many other things that Jesus did; if every one of them were written down, I suppose that the world itself could not contain the books that would be written. (John 21:25, NRSV)*

John gives his own version of the passion story, largely independent of the Synoptic Gospels but also with many parallel accounts. The culmination, of course, is Jesus's crucifixion and death, but John includes many sayings of Jesus that are not found in Matthew, Mark, and Luke. The chronology is similar, beginning with the Last Supper. John says, "The devil had already put it into the heart of Judas son of Simon Iscariot to betray him [Jesus]" (John 13:2). John also includes Jesus's prediction of Peter's denials (vv. 36-38). Many sayings of Jesus follow in chapters 14, 15, 16, and 17. Thus, the Last Supper and sayings of Jesus comprise five chapters of the passion story in John. Chapters 18 and 19 tell of Jesus's arrest, trial, crucifixion, and burial.

What follows here are the events and sayings in John's story of the passion of Christ. I'm using the headings from *The Learning Bible*, Contemporary English Version, with the verses from John listed and the parallel passages, when applicable, from the Synoptic Gospels in parentheses.

JESUS WASHES THE FEET OF HIS DISCIPLES
John 13:1-18

Washing the feet of dinner guests was usually performed by a servant of the host. Jesus, to the astonishment of his disciples, took on that servant role and washed their feet. The foot washing was symbolic of what was to come—Jesus laying down his life and dying on the cross for the sins of the world. Initially, Simon Peter objected to Jesus washing his feet. Jesus told him that "you really don't know what I am doing, but later you will understand" (John 3:7, CEV). Jesus then told them that what he was doing was an example of what they should do for one another.

JESUS TELLS WHAT WILL HAPPEN TO HIM
John 13:21-30 (Matthew 26:20-25; Mark 14:17-21; Luke 22:21-23)

Jesus predicted that one of them would betray him. Jesus dipped a piece of bread into the sauce and gave it to Judas, son of Simon Iscariot. At that moment Satan took control of Judas, and Judas took the piece of bread and left. The other disciples assumed Judas was going to buy something for the festival since he was in charge of the money. John concluded, "it was already night" (John 13:30b, CEV).

THE NEW COMMAND
John 13:31-35

After Judas had left, Jesus gave his disciples a new command to love each other just as he had loved them. Jesus concluded, "If you love each other, everyone will know that you are my disciples" (John 13:35, CEV).

PETER'S PROMISE
John 13:36-38 (Matthew 26:31-35; Mark 14:27-31; Luke 22:31-34)

Peter promised that he would be willing to die for Jesus. In response, Jesus predicted that before a rooster crowed, Peter would deny Jesus three times, saying that he didn't even know Jesus.

JESUS IS THE WAY TO THE FATHER
John 14:1-14

Jesus told his disciples to have faith, to believe in God, and to believe in him. He said there are many rooms in his Father's house. Jesus was going there to prepare a place for each of them. The disciple Thomas replied, "Lord, we don't even know where you are going! How can we know the way?" Jesus answered, "I am the way, the truth, and the life! Without me, no one can go to the Father." The disciple Philip said, "Lord, show us the Father" (John 14:5-6, 8 CEV). Then Jesus explained that he was one with the Father.

THE HOLY SPIRIT IS PROMISED
John 14:15-31

Jesus promised to send the Holy Spirit to be with them. The Holy Spirit is God's presence among us. Thus, Jesus would not leave them like orphans. He would come back to them. Another disciple named Judas (not Judas Iscariot) asked Jesus to explain what he was saying. Jesus replied that God would send the Holy Spirit to them to take his place. Jesus promised to give them peace. This peace would be more than the absence of conflict. It would sustain them even after Jesus was gone.

JESUS IS THE TRUE VINE
John 15:1-17

Jesus used a vine as a metaphor to explain his connection with the disciples and their connection to him. As branches on the vine, they would produce the fruit of love for God and love for other people. Jesus told them to love each other as he had loved them.

THE WORLD'S HATRED
JOHN 15:18-16:4

Jesus warned the disciples that people would mistreat them as they had mistreated Jesus. People would do to them what they were going to do to him. But Jesus would send the Spirit to help them. He told them this to keep them from being afraid when were persecuted for following him.

THE WORK OF THE HOLY SPIRIT
John 16:4b-15

Jesus promised the disciples that the Holy Spirit would come to help them after he was gone.

SORROW WILL TURN INTO JOY
John 16:16-33

Jesus knew that the disciples didn't understand about the coming struggles. They too would suffer, but their sorrow would turn into joy because Jesus overcame the world.

JESUS PRAYS
John 17

Jesus prays for himself and for his followers.

JESUS IS BETRAYED AND ARRESTED
John 18:1-11 (Matthew 26:47-56; Mark 14:43-50; Luke 22:47-53)

When Jesus finished praying, he went with his disciples across the Kidron Valley to a garden. Because Jesus had often convened with his disciples there, Judas knew the place. Judas led Roman soldiers and temple police to arrest Jesus. Simon Peter sought to defend Jesus with a sword. Peter struck the servant of the high priest, cutting off his ear. The servant's name was Malchus. Jesus told Peter to put away his sword.

JESUS IS BROUGHT TO ANNAS
John 18:12-14 (Matthew 26:57; Mark 14:53,54; Luke 22:54)

Annas was the father-in-law of the high priest, Caiaphas. After they had arrested Jesus and tied him up, the Roman officer and his men, along with the temple police, brought Jesus to Annas. Annas was no longer the high priest officially, but he was consulted on major issues, such as what to do with Jesus.

PETER SAYS HE DOESN'T KNOW JESUS
John 18:15-18 (Matthew 26:69, 70; Mark 14:66-68; Luke 22:55-57)

Simon Peter and another disciple (probably John himself) followed Jesus after his arrest into the courtyard of the high priest. Because the other disciple knew the high priest, he was granted entrance into the courtyard, and he spoke to the girl at the gate to grant Peter access as well. The girl asked Peter, "Aren't you one of his followers?" Peter denied it. Seeing that the servants and temple police had made a charcoal fire to warm themselves, Peter went near the fire to warm himself.

JESUS IS QUESTIONED BY THE HIGH PRIEST
John 18:19-24 (Matthew 26:59-66; Mark 14:55-64; Luke 22:66-71)

Annas sent Jesus to Caiaphas after questioning him. One of the temple police struck Jesus for being disrespectful to Annas. Jesus was still tied up when he was hit. So much for the religious leaders!

PETER AGAIN DENIES THAT HE KNOWS JESUS
John 18:23-27 (Matthew 26:71-75; Mark 14:69-72; Luke 22:58-62)

While warming himself, Peter was twice more accused of being a follower of Jesus. One of the accusers was a relative of the servant whose ear Peter had sliced off. Again, Peter denied it, and a rooster crowed.

JESUS IS TRIED BY PILATE
John 18:28-38 (Matthew 27:1-2, 11-14; Mark 15:1-5; Luke 23:1-5)

Pilate asked Jesus if he was the king of the Jews. Jesus answered, "My kingdom is not of this world." Pilate didn't understand. He asked, "What is truth?"

JESUS IS SENTENCED TO DEATH
John 18:38b-19:16 (Matthew 27:15-31; Mark 15:6-20; Luke 23:13-25)

Pilate said he did not find Jesus guilty of anything. Since Pilate usually would release a prisoner at Passover, he offered to release Jesus. The crowd shouted, "No, we want Barabbas." Barabbas was a terrorist. Pilate ordered Jesus to be beaten with a whip. Soldiers made a crown of thorns and put it on Jesus's head. They also beat Jesus with their fists. Pilate still did not find Jesus guilty and wanted to set him free. But the crowds and chief priests demanded that Jesus be nailed to a cross. So Pilate handed him over to be crucified.

JESUS IS NAILED TO A CROSS
John 19:16b-27 (Matthew 27:32-44; Mark 15:21-32; Luke 23:26-43)

Jesus carried his cross to Golgotha, where the soldiers nailed him to it. There is no mention of Simon of Cyrene carrying the cross part of the way. Pilate ordered the charge against Jesus to be written on a board and placed on the cross over Jesus's head. The charge read, "Jesus of Nazareth, King of the Jews," written in Hebrew, Latin, and Greek. The chief priests objected to Pilate naming Jesus "King of the Jews," but Pilate would not change the label. The soldiers divided Jesus's clothing among themselves by lot. Jesus's mother and her sister were there, along with his beloved disciple, presumably John. Jesus entrusted his mother and John to each other.

THE DEATH OF JESUS
John 19:28-30 (Matthew 27:45-56; Mark 15:33-41; Luke 23:44-49)

Jesus said from the cross, "I'm thirsty." Someone soaked a sponge with cheap wine and held it up to Jesus's mouth. After he took the wine he said, "It's finished," and bowed his head and died.

A SPEAR IS STUCK IN JESUS'S SIDE
John 19:31-37

So that Jesus and the two men crucified alongside him did not remain on their crosses on the Sabbath, the Jewish leaders asked Pilate to have the men's legs broken and their bodies taken down. The soldiers broke the legs of the two other men, but since Jesus was already dead, they did not break his legs. One of the soldiers stuck a spear in Jesus's side. Having no broken bones and being pierced with a spear fulfilled prophesies in Exodus 12:46; Numbers 9:12; Psalm 34:20; and Zechariah 12:10.

JESUS IS BURIED
John 19:38-42 (Matthew 27:57-61; Mark 15:42-47; Luke 23:50-56)

A secret disciple, Joseph of Arimathea, and another secret disciple, Nicodemus, buried Jesus. Joseph asked Pilate for the body, and he took it down from the cross. Nicodemus provided seventy-five pounds of spices. Together they wrapped the body in a linen cloth, along with the spices, and laid the body in a nearby tomb that had never been used. They did it in a hurry, since the Sabbath was fast approaching.

The passion story in John's Gospel, then, parallels many of the accounts in the Synoptic Gospels, but John adds additional details and provides many of Jesus's sayings. John also provides insight into Jesus's relationships, especially with his mother.

MARY, THE MOTHER OF JESUS
John 19:25b-27

Jesus had a complicated relationship with his mother. Or maybe Mary had a complicated relationship with her son. However I say it, their relationship was complicated. Let me explain what I mean.

To study their relationship, I looked at all the passages in the New Testament where the mother of Jesus is mentioned. There are not as many as you might think. Mark's Gospel contains just two passages. In Mark 3:31-35 (NRSV), we read, "Then his mother and his brothers came; and standing outside, they sent to him and called him." Someone told him, "Your mother and your brothers are outside, asking for you." Jesus gave a surprising response. He replied, "Who are my mother and my brothers?" Then, looking at those who were sitting around him, he said, "Here are my mother and my brothers! Whoever does the will of God is my brother and sister and mother.

The only other place where Mark mentions the mother of Jesus is in chapter 6. Jesus had come to his hometown and was teaching on the Sabbath. Many who heard him were astounded. They said, "Is not this the carpenter, the son of Mary and brother of James and Joses and Judas and Simon, and are not his sisters here with us?" (v. 3). Mary does not actually appear in this passage, but she is mentioned by name.

So Mark's Gospel does not offer much about the relationship between Jesus and his mother. At one point during his public ministry, his mother and brothers came to speak with him, and Jesus seems to have rebuffed them or at least delayed talking with them. He made the surprising comment that whoever does the will of God is his mother and sister and brother. In the other instance, the people of Nazareth were incredulous about Jesus because they knew his family, the common folks he came from.

Matthew repeats the same two incidents in his Gospel. But Matthew adds stories about Mary surrounding the birth and infancy of Jesus. First, Matthew says in chapter 1 that Mary was engaged to Joseph, and before they lived together, "she was found to be with child from the Holy Spirit" (Matt 1:18, NRSV). "Joseph, being a righteous man and unwilling to expose her to public disgrace, planned to dismiss her quietly" (1:19). Joseph wanted to save Mary the humiliation of being labeled an adulteress, since her pregnancy would have been viewed as a moral failure on her part. Then Joseph learned in a dream that the child conceived in her was from the Holy Spirit, and he should not be afraid to take Mary as his wife.

Matthew also tells us about the visit of the wise men after Jesus was born in Bethlehem: "On entering the house, they saw the child with Mary his mother; and they knelt down and paid him homage" (2:11). Immediately following the visit

The Passion Story in John

of the wise men, Joseph took the child and his mother to Egypt, being warned in a dream that King Herod was about to search for the child to destroy him. Then, after receiving messages from God in two more dreams, Joseph returned with the child and his mother to his hometown of Nazareth to live there.

So far, we still don't know much about the relationship between Jesus and his mother. But it gets more interesting in Luke's Gospel, especially in the first two chapters. In chapter 1 we are told about the annunciation to the virgin Mary, when the angel Gabriel appeared to her in Nazareth with the incredible news that the Holy Spirit would come upon her and she would conceive and bear a son. Since she was not yet married, such a pregnancy would no doubt be seen as scandalous. Still, Mary answered, "Hear am I, the servant of the Lord" (Luke 1:38).

Next, pregnant Mary visited her cousin Elizabeth, who was also with child. After learning that the child in Elizabeth's womb leaped for joy at the sound of her greeting, Mary offered a song of praise to God, beginning, "My soul magnifies the Lord" (v. 46).

After spending three months with Elizabeth (v. 56), Mary traveled with Joseph to Bethlehem to be registered by the government. While there Mary gave birth to Jesus and laid him in a manger, because there was no place for them in the inn. Shepherds came from the fields to see what had been told them by angels about the birth of a Savior. After hearing the report of the shepherds, Mary "treasured all these words and pondered them in her heart" (2:19).

At the appropriate time, Mary and Joseph took the infant Jesus to the temple in Jerusalem to present him to the Lord. A righteous man in the temple named Simeon took the baby in his arms and offered a blessing to God. The child's father and mother were amazed at what Simeon said about him. Then Simeon said to Mary, "This child is destined for the falling and rising of many in Israel…and a sword will pierce your own soul too" (2:34-35).

Finally, Luke tells us about one other episode when Jesus was twelve years old. His parents took him to Jerusalem for the Passover. On their way home after the festival, his parents discovered Jesus was not with the traveling party. Mary and Joseph returned to Jerusalem to search for him. They were astonished to find him in the temple, sitting among the teachers, listening, and asking them questions. His mother said to Jesus, "Child, why have you treated us like this? Look, your father and I have been searching for you in great anxiety" (Luke 2:48). Jesus said to them, "Why were you searching for me? Did you not know that I must be in my Father's house?" (v. 49). His parents didn't understand what he was saying. But they returned together to Nazareth, and Jesus was obedient to them. Once again, his mother treasured all these things in her heart. Luke presents Mary as a woman who was at times perplexed and amazed at being the mother of Jesus.

In John's Gospel, the complexity of the relationship between Jesus and his mother comes most clearly into view. Mary appears in John only after Jesus is an adult beginning his public ministry. She is with Jesus and his disciples as guests at a wedding in Cana, and she says to him, "they have no wine" (John 2:3). It's a potentially embarrassing situation, and she wants Jesus to do something about it. At first Jesus seems to balk. He says to his mother, "Woman, what concern is that to you and to me? My hour has not yet come" (v. 4). Mary seems to ignore Jesus's reluctance to get involved. She says to the servants, "Do whatever he tells you" (v. 5). Despite his apparent initial disinterest, Jesus does do something. He turns water into wine in the first of his signs that revealed his glory.

The only other interaction in John's Gospel between Jesus and his mother happens when Jesus is dying on the cross. His mother is there, along with some other women and the beloved disciple (presumably John himself). Seeing his mother and the disciple he loved, Jesus said, "'Woman, here is your son.' Then he said to the disciple, 'Here is your mother'" (John 19:26-27). The disciple took Mary into his own home. Thus, one of Jesus's last acts from the cross was to make sure his mother would be cared for. Mary had other children who presumably could have taken care of her, but they did not yet understand who Jesus was. It was only after the resurrection that the brothers of Jesus came to believe in him.

The final mention of the mother of Jesus is in the book of Acts, also written by Luke. Acts 1:14 says that after Jesus had ascended into heaven, the disciples devoted themselves to prayer, "along with certain women, including Mary the mother of Jesus, as well as his brothers." Mary and his brothers joined with other women and the disciples in praying together after the risen Jesus was no longer with them in bodily form. So Mary and his brothers (and perhaps his sisters) became believers too.

I have noted that the relationship between Jesus and his mother was complicated. At first, Mary struggled to understand what Jesus was all about. She knew he was the Son of God, but she did not fully understand what that meant. Yet Mary continued to love Jesus with a mother's love. And Jesus continued to love her to the very end.

The relationship between Jesus and his mother is a model for all children and parents. We may not always understand each other, but we can always love each other. There may be times when we are not exactly in agreement, but the love is always there.

Mothers and children may not always see eye to eye. Even Jesus and his mother had their disagreements. Remember Jesus as a precocious twelve-year-old in the temple, when his mother reprimanded him for causing them anxiety. Remember the wedding at Cana, when Jesus seemed reluctant to do what his mother asked him and then did it anyway. Remember Jesus teaching the crowds and seeming put off when his mother and brothers came to talk to him, as if he didn't appreciate being interrupted (Matt 12:46-50). Yet, in the end, Jesus and his mother were there for each other. Mary was there when Jesus was dying on the cross, and Jesus made sure his mother would be okay after he was gone.

Mary and Jesus had a complicated relationship, but most importantly, they loved each other and were there for each other. When Jesus could no longer be present for his mother, he made sure the beloved disciple would care for her so Mary would never be alone.

Whatever our family situations, however complicated our relationships may be, may God help us to love each other and be there for each other. Next to loving God, loving each other is the most important thing we can do.

QUESTIONS FOR DISCUSSION/REFLECTION

1. What do you think Mary understood about her son, Jesus?
2. What did Mary not understand about Jesus?
3. Why do you think Jesus entrusted his mother and the beloved disciple to each other?
4. What role did Mary play in the early church?
5. How is the relationship between Jesus and his mother a model for us?

Bibliography

Achtemeier, Paul J., general editor. *HarperCollins Bible Dictionary*. New York: HarperCollins Publishers, 1996.

Durso, Pamela R., and Keith E. Durso. *The Story of Baptists in the United States*. Brentwood, TN: Baptist History and Heritage Society, 2006.

Lamott, Anne. *Traveling Mercies: Some Thoughts on Faith*. New York: Pantheon Books, 1999.

McCord, T. B., Jr. *Across the Fence But a World Apart. The Coleman Site, 1796–1907*. Alexandria, VA: Alexandria Urban Archaeology Program, 1985.

Moltmann, Jürgen. *The Crucified God*. Minneapolis: Fortress Press, 2015.

Sakenfeld, Katharine Doob, General Editor. *The New Interpreter's Dictionary of the Bible*, A-C. Volume 1. Nashville: Abingdon Press, 2006.

Salmon, Bruce C. *Spelunking Scripture: Easter*. Macon, GA: Nurturing Faith, 2022.

———. *The Barefoot Eulogist: Speaking a Good Word While Standing on Holy Ground*. Macon, GA: Nurturing Faith, 2022.

The Learning Bible: Contemporary English Version. New York: American Bible Society, 2000.

Throckmorton, Burton H., Jr., editor. *Gospel Parallels: A Comparison of the Synoptic Gospels*, Fifth Edition. Nashville: Thomas Nelson, Inc., 1992.

Wiesel, Eliezer. *Night*. New York: Hill and Wang, 2006.

Whitaker, Richard E., and John R. Kohlenberger III. *The Analytical Concordance to the New Revised Standard Version of the New Testament*. Grand Rapids, MI: Williams B. Eerdmans Publishing Company, 2000.

About the Author

Bruce Salmon served for thirty-three years as pastor of Village Baptist Church in Bowie, Maryland. During that time, he preached almost 1,500 original Sunday morning sermons, including many sermons on the Passion story. For the last eighteen years of his ministry, he taught a Sunday morning Pastor's Adult Bible Study Class that read and discussed entire books of the Bible. He also led winter, summer, and Lenten Sunday evening adult Bible studies, covering such topics as "Introducing the New Testament," "The Sermon on the Mount," "The Life of Christ," "The Life of Paul," "The Passion of Jesus," and "The Jesus of the Bible," as well as books of the Bible including Hebrews, James, Malachi, John, 2 Corinthians, Acts, Isaiah, Genesis, Exodus, Revelation, Joshua, Mark, Luke, 1 & 2 Samuel, Romans, Ezekiel, and Matthew.

A native of Fort Worth, Texas, Salmon received the Bachelor of Arts with a major in English from Baylor University. He received the Master of Divinity and the Doctor of Ministry degrees from The Southern Baptist Theological Seminary. He also received the Master of Arts in Counseling Psychology from Bowie State University, with a specialization in Clinical Pastoral Counseling. Salmon has served on several committees of the DC Baptist Convention and several commissions of the Baptist World Alliance.

In addition to this volume and the other volumes in this series, *Spelunking Scripture*, he is the author of the books *Storytelling in Preaching*; *Preaching for the Long Haul: A Case Study on Long-term Pastoral Ministry*; and *The Barefoot Eulogist: Speaking a Good Word While Standing on Holy Ground*.

Salmon is husband to wife Linda, father to grown children Amy and Marc, father-in-law to Stacey, and grandfather to granddaughter Ford. In addition to studying the Bible, his interests include spectator sports, music, current events, museums, golf, and travel.

www.ingramcontent.com/pod-product-compliance
Lightning Source LLC
Chambersburg PA
CBHW071007160426
43193CB00012B/1948